DATE DUE			

THE COMING BREAKPOINT

Barry Goldwater

THE COMING BREAKPOINT

Macmillan Publishing Co., Inc.
NEW YORK
Collier Macmillan Publishers
LONDON

Macmillan Publishing Co., Inc.
866 Third Avenue, New York, N.Y. 10022
Collier Macmillan Canada, Ltd.

Library of Congress Cataloging in Publication Data

Goldwater, Barry Morris, 1909–
  The coming breakpoint.
  Includes index.
  1. United States—Executive departments. 2. United States—Politics and government—1933–1945. 3. United States—Politics and government—1945–   4. Bureaucracy. I. Title.
JK421.G63   353   75–38696
ISBN 0–02–544611–8

Second Printing 1976

Printed in the United States of America

CONTENTS

ACKNOWLEDGMENTS

In the Introduction to this book I mention that the Washington Monument reminds us of honesty. In an effort to keep that concept alive in these pages, I want to make the usual confession that I insert in every work that bears my name: This book is not the product solely of my pen or my typewriter or my dictating machine. There were others who helped me, others on whom I leaned for advice, ideas, suggestions, and corrections. Chief among these people were my press secrtary of many, many years, Mr. Tony Smith, and, of course, his staff; my devoted secretary of over twenty years, Mrs. Earl Eisenhower, whom we call Judy; and my legislative assistant, Mr. Terry Emerson.

Introduction

I hope I can convey to the reader of this book the deep concern I feel about the direction in which our country has been heading for too long a time.

In stark terms, our economic survival is being jeopardized, and the question facing us is whether the working population of America can indefinitely carry an ever-increasing burden of government spending to support the nonworking segment of our society.

If we continue on our present course, with annual enlargements of the welfare state, we will inevitably reach a *breakpoint*—a place in time where the taxpayers' ability to withstand the load of unlimited government largesse finally gives way. We are rushing toward that breakpoint at blinding speed. If we reach it before effective stop measures are adopted, we could see our Republic collapse and our democracy smother to death under a mountain of government debt, regulation, and red tape.

The frightening thing about the whole situation is the realization of how few responsible people there are, in and out of government, who actually know what is happening. Occasionally, a voice is raised in alarm, but it is either ignored or forgotten in a matter of hours. The most concerned are those who have had a close look at the overall picture of government operations. For example, former

Secretary of the Department of Health, Education and
Welfare Caspar Weinberger has warned that the nation's
growing welfare system, all by itself, threatens the country
with bankruptcy. And Roy L. Ash, former director of the
Federal Office of Management and Budget, said in an article
in the *Wall Street Journal* that if we continue as we have
been, government at all levels will command well over half
of this country's gross national product in just twenty-five
years—in other words, it will appropriate 50 percent of the
proceeds of all the business, commercial, industrial, and
financial activity of all the people and groups in the United
States.

Ash concludes: "I believe we stand at a watershed point
right now on decisions that could be central in determining
the kind of social and political system we will have, not
just in our children's time but in our own time."

And it is against the backdrop of *the coming breakpoint*
that one of the most fundamental issues in the entire history of America has taken shape and is ready for debate:
the tremendous concentration of power in the hands of
government bureaucrats and the abuse of that power in the
handling of the people's affairs.

One of the purposes of this book is to outline the dimensions of that debate, and in so doing, to detail in a brief
way the derivation of our concepts of government and freedom, and to call attention to the destruction being wrought
by the power structure on what most particularly concerns
me—the freedoms of the individual or, to put it on a more
personal basis, the freedoms of you, the reader.

I sense an air of finality about the power structure's
effort which compels me—reluctantly—to confess that the
events of the past year have made me wonder, for the very
first time, whether we are equal to making our system of

government meet and overcome the challenges and tasks that lie ahead. If we are not, then we may be witnessing the "last hurrah" of the American system of government based on ordered justice.

I desperately wish I could sound an optimistic note. But the fact of the matter is that any political currency I have with the American people stems from my habitual candor. My practice in public has always been to "tell it like it is." Call it a trademark, if you will, but I do believe this trait, which is characteristic of almost a way of life in Arizona and other parts of the Far West, is the "extra something" which many times has set me somewhat apart from my colleagues in the Congress. Of course, it has cost me votes and friendships now and then, just as it has gained me some of my most cherished lifelong associations. My public frankness hurt me deeply (and I mean that in a political sense) when I ran for the office of president of the United States on the Republican ticket of 1964. At almost every turn, someone was urging political expediency on me as a vote-getting device, and some of my best friends could not understand why it was impossible for me to change. Expediency has its points—that I can admit very freely—but I also know from long experience that it is not equal to the plain, unvarnished truth, whether it be in politics or any other line of human endeavor.

Having made this clear, I believe it is time to tell the American people that economically, morally, materially, and otherwise, our country is in the kind of deep trouble that has been known to touch off worldwide depressions and wars. And what bothers me most is that while the trouble was building up, nobody seemed to have the slightest idea of what to do about it, when to do it, or where to find the courage to do it. Some sound suggestions were made but the Congress seemed to lack the fortitude to act upon them.

For almost two decades I, along with other conservatives, have been warning the United States that it was following the same course every other nation had taken before it collapsed and became just another tombstone along the road of history. Now that the day of reckoning is actually bearing down on us, I dearly wish my responsibility was at an end. Certainly, I would derive no satisfaction from saying, "I told you so," but I do wish I could forget all that is happening and sit out the rest of my years on my beloved hill in Arizona.

But I can't do that. If ever there was a time for the advocates of the economy and constitutional government to do what they can to help avert total disaster, this is it. And if ever there was a time for publicly identifying the pockets of power in the bureaucracy, with their accompanying threat to individual freedom, this is it. The economic situation facing the United States is just short of desperate and one of the things the nation needs most is the help and advice of those in Congress and in government who have spent years fighting for balanced budgets, reduced government spending, payments on the national debt, and a tough-minded policy toward those sweet-sounding but expensive programs of social engineering. We also need the help of like-minded people in electing Congresses with the courage to act in the interests of all Americans.

In the years when the full effect of policy foolishness was starting to be recognized, the liberals—because it was the easiest and most politically popular course—pooh-poohed the fears and warnings of those who called for a halt to reckless spending and pie-in-the-sky schemes. So convincing were they that most previously concerned Americans were lulled into believing that their apprehensions were groundless. Now we know differently.

Tragically, the devastation caused by years of deficit spending and abuse of power (most of it concentrated in the federal government and individuals) under the guise of the welfare state shows every sign of coinciding with our celebration of the 200th birthday of the Republic.

Most federal officials, and a great many congressmen and senators, know the true state of affairs and have known it for some time, but most of them appear afflicted with a strange disease that manifests itself in a conviction that the American people should not know the truth or that "it can't happen here."

It doesn't help any, but it is ironic to realize that the trouble we presently face was the work of the "big spenders" in Congress who right now are raising the chant about the "public's right to know" every detail of every sordid mess hinted at by the news media, but who do not want the truth about our economic situation exposed either at home or abroad.

One of my reasons for writing this book is that I believe this is no time for the American people to be hoodwinked by still another double standard established by public officials, members of Congress, or the news media. Americans have the guts to take the bad news and the intelligence to do what is necessary to reverse our downward trend. This has been proven time and time again throughout the two-hundred-year history of this country, yet everyone, especially those in the new Administration, tiptoes around as though the opposite were true. But I repeat, the American public can take it—the trouble is that for months on end nobody has told them just what they will have to take.

Yes, I know all the arguments against this kind of painful

forthrightness. But none of them offers any justification for withholding the truth from American citizens, especially since to do so, for all my critics know, could actually be a life-and-death matter.

Think about it for a minute: The citizens of the United States support with their hard-earned dollars all the governments—federal, state, and local—that exist in this country. Consider that in times of war many of those taxpayers have given their blood, risked their lives, or sustained horrible injuries to protect our freedom on the field of battle. And it would help to remember that many of them made these sacrifices in the belief that the rest of us, as well as our children and grandchildren, would be better able to enjoy the fruits of freedom devised by the wise men who wrote our Constitution.

Don't people such as these have the right to know the bad news as well as the good? Should only a select group of our countrymen, arbitrarily chosen, have the kind of knowledge that may be required to protect their own future and the future of their families?

In World War II one of our finer generals said to the Germans when they asked him to surrender, "Nuts!" And I say just that today to those who fear the American people don't have what it takes to measure up to the difficulties and discomforts that they will have to undergo if the nation is to be put back on an even keel.

Who in this country is so important that he can comfortably arrogate to himself the privilege of deciding who among us is strong enough to handle bad news and its implications? In my considered opinion, no one is that important—certainly not the author of this book; certainly not the leaders of Congress or the "think-tank" crew at the White House.

of continuing progress and freedom is a question of relativity. What I am saying is that in deciding a question so vital, it is absolutely essential to find out how the rest of the world is doing. And I am not talking merely about the free world. I think we have to assess what goes on in Eastern Europe and the Soviet Union as well as on the mainland of China.

That America still represents a beacon of freedom to the oppressed peoples of the world is a view so widely accepted that it can be had from any place on the compass. Much the same can be said for the old but cherished cliché that America is the land of opportunity; that to the needy, she is the land of plenty; to the statesman, the land of noble experiment; to the free and would-be free throughout the world, always and everywhere a friend.

Interestingly enough, the founders of America never saw her in terms of wealth or power or size, or even of individual freedom and equality. Instead, I think it is accurate to say that the men who made government history by actually writing a constitution of, by, and for the people never saw their work in anything but terms of simple honor and freedom. They used freedom as the pivot against which power in government is aimed.

I suspect that in the founders' perspective, America was seen as a governmental device propped up by the honor and integrity of her citizens as much as by anything else. This is a concept that says a great deal about our nation and about ourselves. It even gives a certain substance and definition to the clichés we use to describe ourselves.

We were meant to be a government of laws, but one of the laws is that all the others should be honored—that is, both obeyed and revered—by those who write them, by those who implement them, and by those who live with them. At any time when this condition does not prevail, then we have ceased being America and have become a government of men.

Understand me well. There is nothing about our laws that compels us to honor them or prevents us from dishonoring them—except the penalties written into those laws. By and large the laws of this land are just in most respects, and there is nothing about our system of enforcement that would validate a policy of ignoring them. America is truly a contrivance of honor and it holds together only so long as the cement adheres.

That cement has weakened over the past four decades through the ascendancy of an executive bureaucratic organization so extensive that no one person can actually define its limits in precise terms. And here we encounter the seeds of government disaster and collapse—the kind that wrecked ancient Rome and every other civilization that allowed a sociopolitical monster called the welfare state to exist.

One of the greatest and most enduring thrills of my life is that of flying into the nation's capital and seeing two outstanding landmarks—the Washington Monument and the Capitol dome. At night they are well lighted and can be seen for some distance when coming in to land at either Washington National Airport or Andrews Air Force Base.

The Washington Monument was erected to remind us of the greatness and honesty of our first president. Every time I see it, I am stricken with a kind of historic awe when I realize that it looks down upon the greatest "powerhouse" in the Western world.

Behind all the facade, the beautiful buildings, the works of art, the cherry blossoms, and the magnificent structures such as the Lincoln Memorial, there runs a machine of government which reaches around the world, pumping power and influence into the smallest nooks and crannies. Few Americans realize the extent of the power that streams from Washington, D.C., into their lives and into the businesses of everyone in the free world. The city, often simply called "the nation's capital," has also been termed "the news center of the world." Some people call it America's most beautiful city. But its real importance is in the enormous power it wields over every man, woman, and child in this country from the cradle to the grave. It calls the turn on billions of dollars in contracts. It calls the turn on millions upon millions of jobs. It is the place where wars are declared and where food airlifts to starving nations originate. And this doesn't even begin to tell the whole story.

The Capitol dome doesn't remind us of anything in particular but, rather, of the whole wonderful concept of our government. However, during the past several years we have been learning of some very distasteful, dishonest, unethical, and immoral practices that have gone on in high places in the nation's capital. Now maybe it is time to take a peek under the great dome where the two Houses of Congress sit, debate, and make decisions to see how power is used and/or abused there and to get a better understanding of procedures such as the seniority system of committee assignments that do not always provide the best leadership or the best legislation.

In the course of this book I shall also define the power wielded by the enormous federal bureaucracy, by the Congress through its committee chairmen, by the labor unions, the regulatory agencies, the intellectuals, the "do-gooders," the news media, the educators, and the civil libertarians.

Of course, not the least of these to be discussed will be the bureaucracy, and since nothing like it has ever before existed in the history of the world, this won't be easy. But we can consider matters such as where the enormous grants of power to the executive came from, when they came, and why. We can try to show how the system works. For example, the vast authority of independent agencies to issue regulations which carry the force of law can—and should —be examined.

The power of Congress means a lot more than the mere statement that it exists. I believe the American people will be astounded to know about the authority wielded by committee chairmen as well as their staffs. But know it they shall, regardless of what kind of reaction the disclosure generates.

In short, we have too many convenient rugs in the federal establishment under which the bureaucrats can brush their waste, inefficiency, and corruption. It's time to roll back the rugs to see what they've been concealing. Watergate didn't do the job; neither will any other scandal, even another of like proportions.

As I write these words, I can almost hear the professional liberals in Congress accusing me of being a prophet of doom. On this charge I'd like to engage in some "plea bargaining" (which seems to be a necessarily popular sport among politicians these days) with the radicals on the left: I'll willingly plead guilty to the charge of being a prophet of doom IF the radical-liberal Democrats who control the Congress will stop spending the taxpayers' money on useless boondoggles and social-engineering projects of unproven value.

Another argument I hear from the "professional spenders" on Capitol Hill is that "we" (meaning the United

States and all its citizens) always "muddle through" no matter how serious the problem. This has happened in America in the past. And it has happened in other countries, at least for a considerable period of time. "Muddling through" worked during the plush, irresponsible years of bread and circuses in ancient Rome; it worked in Austria in the 1920s, when that country was building a huge welfare state. But in both Rome and Austria there came a day which could not be muddled through, and as a result, their economies and their governments collapsed under the weight of their own spending and promises. Therefore our ability to muddle through difficult periods in our past does not necessarily mean that we are sure to muddle through the problems facing us today. I wish it did.

Before getting into Chapter I, let me explain again that my purpose in this book is to show what kind of government and what kind of society the Founding Fathers had in mind for the United States when they wrote the Constitution and what has happened to their intentions in the years embraced by the welfare state.

I believe the time has come to tell the American people exactly when and where we went wrong, thus creating the political power crisis that faces the United States today. We must all be in full possession of the facts if we are ever to be able to answer the question: Is man—as man is now constituted—able to govern himself successfully over an extended period of time? The Romans did it for five hundred years; we have just reached our 200th birthday.

In rereading the preceding and following pages, I find that I have occasionally repeated myself. I have allowed these slips to remain because I believe in the power of repetition to stress certain points.

I/ A Contrivance of Honor

Britain's Edmund Burke once defined the government of the United States as a "contrivance of human wisdom to supply the needs of human beings." Needless to say, I believe the plans laid out by the Founding Fathers for our government were all of that—and something more. I believe our forefathers used as much human wisdom as any men had ever put into a project of this kind—the building of a charter for the governing of a people—and in so doing provided us with protection of our God-given freedoms such as no people before have ever enjoyed.

But I honestly believe that these men were motivated by something beyond wisdom that they incorporated in those historic words which we call the U.S. Constitution. Call it what you will, I like the word "spirit," and I believe that spirit can best be exemplified today by the honor which men sworn to uphold the Constitution bring to their task. Trouble enters when such men disregard honor and abuse the powers given them. That was our trouble in the Watergate situation.

I know our forefathers, when they were busy writing with those ridiculous quill pens, really recognized that they were engaged upon a new departure, that they were men plowing new ground in the age-old art of statecraft. I believe they knew full well that in the dusty, faded document that we know today as the Constitution, something new was being added; that the sacred status of the individual human being was being treated in a way men had never known before.

An attempt to get at this spirit of freedom permeating the Constitution has led me to use the word "honor" in the title of this chapter. It is an effort—albeit a clumsy one—to state my honest conviction that there is something about the history of the circumstances, the novelty of the words employed, and the freshness of the attitudes of our fore-fathers (as well as of everyone else connected with the framing, enactment, and adherence to the Constitution's principles) that today demands of those called to serve its government that they perform at their honorable best.

In our contrivance, as in all other governments throughout the world, man is the problem which must be taken into consideration first, last, and always. Man was not contrived with immortality and perfection. I believe it was and is God's purpose to afford all men an opportunity to overcome their inherent differences so that each can strive to make of himself a better person and in so doing rid the world of the evils that breed wars, misunderstandings, and worst of all, discrimination in all its forms.

Like a coin, human nature has two sides—the good and the bad. As I have often noted, if man could keep the good side of the coin up, he would accomplish God's purpose.

Almost sixteen years ago, in my book *The Conscience of a Conservative,* I concentrated on the fact that every man is unique and can be governed only by leaders who acknowledge this quality and adopt a philosophy that pro-vides for the development of each individual's potentiali-

ties, instincts, and endowments. Man cannot today—and
never could in the past—be herded into an undifferentiated
mass and consigned to ultimate slavery.

Nor is it possible to pass a law that could control human
nature. Man is a complex creature. He can be noble one
minute and base the next, generous on some occasions and
miserly on others; he is capable of using the word "hate"
in one sentence and the word "love" in the next.

For some reason the good God populated the earth with
human beings, not angels. If He had made us perfect, there
would be no need for governments, for laws would be unnecessary. Men would treat each other in the way their
Creator intended—as equals in everything they did or
tried to do. There would be no need for anyone ever to
quote the Golden Rule because "Do unto others as you
would have them do unto you" would no longer be an
injunction, but merely a description of what man was doing
naturally.

But it didn't happen that way, and our founders took
man's two-sided nature into account when fashioning a
government to provide the majority of our people with a
system of ordered justice.

One of the most dangerous practices I have run into
since coming to Washington as a senator has been that of
intelligent, highly educated men and women absolutely
refusing to heed the lessons of history. Every day I drive
past the National Archives Building and each time I automatically read the words inscribed on either side of that
building's entrance: "What is past is prologue—study the
past." I often think of this inscription as I sit in the Senate
and listen to debates by men who I know have as much
knowledge of history as I have, and I wonder why they
cannot understand that everything we are doing was done

previously at some point in the history of mankind. And always with the same results—some good; some bad.

I wonder why these members of Congress overlook the vital fact that nations and governments and cultures and civilizations have fallen when power was allowed to gather in the hands of a few, and continue to vote more and more power into the hands of the select few who run the many bureaus of our government. From the days of Hammurabi, this has been a sure road to ruin. These bureaus and agencies formed because Congresses in the past, refusing to take the responsibility for solving problems, merely turned them over to an assemblage of people who, while perfectly honorable and devoted to America, were unaware that a concentration of power has always marked the destruction of the people's efforts to govern themselves.

I wonder, too, as I sit listening in the Senate in these trying times, why the members of Congress cannot remember how it was when the world fell into the Great Depression of the 1930s. The collapse was triggered by the failure of the Kredit-Anstadt, the largest bank in Austria, founded in 1855 by the Rothschilds. Its assets and liabilities amounted to 70 percent of the total of all Austrian banks combined. But even with the Rothschilds' backing, the Kredit-Anstadt could not withstand the strain of the welfare state operating in that country in the late twenties. If the accounts we read are true, there were so many subsidies, they could scarcely be counted. Austria had public housing, public schooling, public health care, public transportation, and many, many other programs typical of a government which wants to rule its people from the cradle to the grave.

But all this seems to have been forgotten in the midst of the economic difficulties that are engulfing the world today.

Listen to the experts all you want. Right now listen to

the economists wrangling about what should and shall be done about inflation and unemployment. Listen to the politicians, many of whom are merely grinding their axes with rhetoric. But never forget that history is our greatest teacher.

Indeed, what is past *is* prologue. If only the members of Congress would remember this fact and stop trying to deceive themselves and their constituents into believing that everything is new and that old problems can be solved by devices which have always failed!

It should be kept in mind that the framers of the Constitution and the Declaration of Independence went back to the beginning to find their building materials. They reached a conviction that the simple fact of man's birth—the mere entrance of an individual into the human race—of and by itself marked that individual as the most important of God's earthly creations. And having decided this, our forefathers agreed that *all* men were born equal and thereby endowed with certain God-given—not man-given—rights automatically entitling them to a certain dignity and respect which they could carry into their meetings and dealings with other human beings. They further agreed that each human being should be free to build his own life without interference from other individuals or groups of individuals.

As I write these words they strike me as dull and mundane enough to warrant comparing the author to a kid taking his first written exam in a high school course on the problems of democracy. But just try to imagine, if you will, how exciting and revolutionary these words of the Declaration of Independence must have struck other statesmen and practitioners of the art of statecraft in nations which had never had or never even considered a government which would be the servant of the governed. And think of how they must have sounded to men all over the globe who yearned for individual freedom.

Undoubtedly, many shook their heads and said, "It will never work." Thomas Jefferson, our third president and our foremost governmental philosopher in the early days of the Republic, regarded the new system of government in the United States as a great experiment which would determine for all times whether or not "men may be trusted to govern themselves without a master."

It was Jefferson, too, who predicted future happiness for Americans if, as he put it, "we can prevent the government from wasting the labors of the people under the pretense of taking care of them."

Viewed against the backdrop of the welfare state (circa 1976), these words have a special and a frightening meaning for American citizens. They involve a matter of such enormous importance that it will be dealt with in considerable length later on in this book. For the moment, it is sufficient to note that Jefferson was an expert on the historical reasons for the demise of past governments and past civilizations. Yet, despite his expertise in the history of government failures, he had great faith in the durability and staying power of the U.S. Constitution.

It should be understood and underscored that we are not speaking here of just any old piece of paper or parchment; rather we are speaking of—and I hope paying tribute to— a document that symbolizes the greatest experiment ever devised to serve the largest number of our people and to afford each and every individual the opportunity to make the most of the gifts and talents with which he was endowed by his Creator. To me that document has always represented the world's most determined governmental attempt

to treat all the people of a country fairly, as well as man's
best effort to construct a system of equity and justice, one
that sees government solely in the role of an agency designed to extend help to the people when it is most sorely
needed. Government's role under such a system should be
to render service to, not exact service from, those who pay
for it and live by its precepts. Its primary responsibility
should be to use as little power as possible to get a job done
for the taxpayers, and even that power should be diffused
as much and as quickly as possible to prevent the seeds of
totalitarianism from growing and catching hold in a way
that eventually leads to dictatorship.

Let me hasten to add I know full well that there is a
certain amount of power attached to any action, popular or
unpopular, that the government takes or is assigned to
take. This is unavoidable. The best we can do is to make
sure that this power is *not* extended or abused.

Since I firmly believe in honor among politicians, I believe the word "honor" has an important place in any
discussion of governmental action or contribution. It needs
repetition and it needs emphasis, especially in a government
of laws, not men. Actually the best government is one that
governs least, and the best, unfortunately, is no better than
the humans who operate it. I happen to believe that we
have in the United States a superb system of government,
but if it is manned—even for a little while—by persons
who have no respect for the Constitution, the law, or
honor, we are in serious, serious trouble. This has happened a few times over the years. Watergate was the latest
and perhaps the most sensational example. Venal as it was,
however, Watergate is no reason to downgrade and find
fault with the basic system.

In fact, as of now the American system of representative

democracy has never been stronger. It's got to be, in order
to stand up under the kind of beating the Nixon Administration and its critics gave it for over two years. If it hadn't
been for the "contrivance of honor," chances are we might
never have known the full ramifications of the Watergate
break-in. And if it hadn't been for the system our forefathers put together nearly two centuries ago, there is
nothing we could have done about it. This is America—
American freedom, I should say—at its operational best.
Can you imagine a situation of comparable embarrassment
to the Kremlin being publicized and investigated in Mos-
cow? Or Fidel Castro accepting enough blame for a "Cuban
Watergate" to bring about the resignations of his two top
aides, a vice-president, and finally himself? Can you visualize
any totalitarian state forcing its top leaders to make public
hours upon hours of tape-recording transcriptions of their
most intimate governmental conversations?

Of course you can't. And that is why I say that despite
all the alarms we hear on TV and radio and read in our
newspapers, books, and magazines, this is not the twilight
of American freedom. It is a time of testing for our democracy—nobody can deny this. But it is comforting to
know that it is not even the gravest time of testing which
our system has ever encountered.

This nation has had previous scandals, some of which
reached into the Cabinet and the White House, and history
tells us that the United States lived through these troublesome periods without losing its freedom or even its international poise. But even if we had not survived similar
incidents in our past, I would still believe our people are
fully capable of coping with whatever challenge lies ahead.
Many readers will undoubtedly recall Hitler's incessant
claim that Americans were soft and decadent, and there-

fore would not be an important factor in World War II. Well, some of us might have been a little out of shape at that time; but the condition was quickly remedied, and before the war was over, American military men on land, at sea, and in the air had made Mr. Hitler look almost as silly as the moustache he wore. I suspect that during American offensives in Europe and elsewhere, Hitler many times wished he had stuck to his paperhanging and left geopolitics and wars to people who knew what they were all about.

Americans are capable of miscalculations and errors. But they are not capable of surrender or giving in to slavery. In fact, in all the wars I know something about, one of the problems has been in getting our men to acknowledge an impossible military situation so that we could cut losses and regroup to fight another day. I can tell from what I see and hear on my many trips to military academies and military posts, which I have visited as a member of the Senate Armed Services Committee, that this spirit is still being carried on by our young officers.

Throughout our two hundred years of existence, the contrivance of honor I write about has been called many things. Jefferson, as I've mentioned, called it an experiment; lawmakers refer to it as an instrument by which government is created; the legal profession chose to call the Constitution a "giant power-of-attorney" and a "solemn covenant for a government by the consent of the governed." Most of these descriptions turn on the question of power and that is precisely what we face today in the "testing time" brought on by Watergate.

No matter what descriptive phrase is used by the present-day contestants, what we need is an answer to the question: How much sovereign power does the federal government hold under the Constitution? To find the answer, we have to reach back to our very beginnings, to when the United States was in a state of transition and we were about to abandon our original constitution, the Articles of Confederation, and adopt the charter under which we now live that laid the legal groundwork of American freedom.

We like to think of ourselves today in terms of governmental sophistication and maturity. After all, the United States is, or at least has been until very recently, the leader of the entire free world and one of the richest and most powerful nations on earth. But we are still a young entity in the family of nations. Yes, we are influential, powerful, and rich, but we must never forget that we reached the pinnacle very quickly—so quickly, in fact, that we may have missed some lessons in statecraft and history along the way.

We are fond of saying (I said it myself earlier) that the United States is a government of laws, not men. However, that isn't entirely correct. We are primarily a government of laws, but it takes men to supply the "spirit" and "honor" to make the laws work with precision and efficiency and truth.

Historians tell us that Thomas Jefferson looked into the soul of America two hundred years ago and enshrined the qualities of freedom, equality, and power in what has come to be known as the Spirit of '76. He didn't define that spirit as such; rather, he expressed it in words that conveyed its meaning. And those words struck a resonant chord in the hearts of the men of the Revolution, through whose agonies, in battle and in debate, America was born.

The Constitution shaped America by giving a structure to the spirit Jefferson perceived. To use an analogy not, I trust, too imprecise or irreverent, the words of Jefferson took on flesh in the body politic defined and formed by the Constitution of the United States. But a body without spirit is dead. Without honor, the American body politic is without vitality.

So it is with the Republic the Constitution gave us—it is not a self-perpetuating machine but, as we were cautioned at the start, only "a Republic if you can keep it." I repeat, there is nothing about our laws that compels men to obey them. Therefore, there is nothing about our Constitution that prevents men in a position to do so from violating it, ignoring it, dishonoring it.

The Constitution, as structured, contains guarantees against the usurpation of state powers by the federal government. But the history of how we have honored that provision—letting it slowly erode and ignoring it altogether in the last few years—is too well known to need repeating. The Constitution, as a structure, contains guarantees against the accumulation of excessive power in one branch of the federal government at the expense of the other two. But the erosion of that principle through entrusting more and more power and discretion to the president (and more dangerously, to those in what we call the Administration) at least, if not at worst, prompted Watergate.

We have always done these things for a good cause. We have abandoned altogether any constitutional notion of states' rights for such worthy goals as equality of education. We have entrusted to the executive branch extraordinary powers for the purpose of enhancing minority rights or getting through an energy crisis or for the sake of peace, though more recently, when we take them away, we refer to them as war powers. We have done these things willingly and with good intent. But while my conservatism informs me that men are the masters of events, my experience teaches me that men are also influenced by the events and trends that occur around them. In the case of Watergate, it might well be called reaping the whirlwind.

By the 1960s, after we in Congress had been circumventing the laws for years, our constituents, in significant numbers, began to emulate us. They sat in, burned draft cards, fled the draft—always, as we had, for "a good cause"—peace, civil rights, or whatever. By the early seventies there were new demonstrations, new ways to dishonor the laws. This time those involved were teachers, truckers, politicians. Though they struck illegally or demonstrated illegally or acted illegally, they, too, did it for a "higher law" or higher pay or a president's reelection.

There are some who would say this trend is inevitable. I would say only that there is precious little to prevent it, save the mortar which is there to hold our laws and our people together, in a contrivance of honor.

II/The Power Buildup

When the Founding Fathers sat down two hundred years ago to write a new contract of government for the United States, their greatest fear was that a centralized accumulation of power would ultimately destroy their best efforts.

They had learned to fear the arrogance of power. In Europe, where most of them had come from, they had seen authority run rampant over the inherent rights of the people. Their knowledge of history had taught them that one civilization after another had succumbed when government power became concentrated in one place or in one person, so they were determined to formulate a charter of government that would withstand such a dangerous threat. They labored long and hard to build a system of ordered justice, and erected checks and balances to keep it on balance.

The magnificent document that resulted from their efforts, the Constitution, stands—as do similar documents such as the Declaration of Independence, the Emancipation Proclamation, and the Four Freedoms Charter—for Americans as our credentials for active participation in the family of nations. In my opinion all nations need a reason for their existence and their activities. The Royal Family has long been the rallying point as well as the carefully guarded treasure of Great Britain. In the case of the

United States our rallying points and treasures are our national symbols, most notably the American flag. But we must also include the written charters of government which were produced for our nation but which have been used by freedom-loving people everywhere.

Yet today America's federal establishment has become an overbearing, arrogant concentration of raw power. It is the largest business in existence, with a payroll so enormous it takes a committee of the Senate almost full time just to keep track of it; the paperwork alone costs the taxpayers billions of dollars a year.

How did this happen? Well, let's take the Postal Service as an example. In 1971, when the old Post Office Department was changed to the new Postal Service, the lobbyists went to work and slipped in a provision allowing the big postal unions to bargain with the postmaster general on wages. As a result, the salary of a postal clerk has increased 67.6 percent in the last few years. If the postal workers were still paid on a scale comparable to that of other government employees, the savings to that department would have amounted to $1.2 billion dollars this year.

Everywhere you look in the nation's capital there is evidence of the gargantuan federal power. Everywhere you look you see a government bureaucracy so large that nobody ever tries to measure its dimensions any more. And everywhere there is power—federal power—wielded by a group of men and women not elected or even heard of by the public. Thus, bureaucrats who never ran for office, who never received a single vote from the electorate, are busy every day pumping American power around our country and the free world, making it felt in nations, states, cities, and towns throughout the entire globe. This power is something which affects and hurts us all.

When our Founding Fathers deliberately set out to construct a government of laws, not men, they attempted to shelter it under a system whereby the three branches of our government—the executive, legislative, and the judiciary —could balance each other out and prevent the lodgment of undue power in any one segment. And the United States of America, working under this novel Constitution, did extremely well for the first 153 years of its existence. It made democracy an international governmental fad and injected a healthy jolt of idealism and discipline into the affairs of other nations.

Then in 1933, while we were experiencing an economic depression of unusual severity, along came a president who learned the meaning of power and how it could best be used by an executive. What's more, Franklin Delano Roosevelt understood better than most previous presidents where political power in the United States was strongest.

And it was right then that the concentration of power so feared by our founders had its beginning.

That was the period which saw the federal bureaucracy begin to build the greatest governmental superstructure of all times. That was when the enormous power of organized-labor got its start, when social engineering became a costly and burgeoning way of life in the U.S. Government, when the ad hoc authority of regulatory agencies took on the force of law, when a once-powerful Congress meekly turned over its authority to the executive bureaucracy and to the chairmen and staffs of its seniority-blighted committees. When FDR assumed the office of president, the legislative branch literally forced upon him, his cabinet, his bureaus, and his agencies the responsibility for all the nation's problems.

Judging from his record as governor of New York and

his campaign speeches in 1932, nothing was farther from FDR's mind when he first took up residence at 1600 Pennsylvania Avenue than an all-powerful federal government. But the idea began to grow on him almost from the start. For example, it was considered necessary to declare a bank holiday to preserve the nation's solvency on the very day FDR was sworn into office. After that, centralized government, with Washington as its hub, became the order of the day for FDR and his "Brain Trust." The result is what we have today—a centralized government so big it frightens even the men who built it. Washington, D.C. is a power factory of almost unbelievable proportions. It is fueled by more than $350 billion and more than two million jobs.

As mentioned earlier, later on in this book I shall deal more specifically with the Washington power source and what it means to the average American citizen. For the present, it is enough to touch on the dimensions of the power concentration, explaining briefly how it came about and showing how far we have moved from the basic intentions of the Founding Fathers when they wrote the Constitution.

I must say it is difficult for me to assess the reasons why the American people—blessed as they have been with liberty and the idea that liberty and freedom are gifts from God— have permitted the concentration of power and the restraints it places on individual action. All around us we see evidence of a decline in morality, ethics, and responsibility to our form of government and the freedom and enterprise which it encompasses. Frankly, I do not fear communism nearly so much as I fear this decline, and, even if the desire to do so exists, the lack of any effort to stop it at the executive or congressional levels.

In recent months I have spent a good deal of time re-

flecting on the past forty years of our history, trying to
determine what they have involved for the American
people. For example, I think about what has happened
since Franklin D. Roosevelt was president and what some
of us might have done, had we been so inclined, to change
the course of events.

In the early days of the New Deal we heard a lot of talk
about a redistribution of the nation's wealth. I believe
many politicians went around the country mouthing that
phrase without ever realizing what it might mean for this
country in the near or distant future. The conclusion I
have come to is that what FDR was involved in was a
deliberate attempt to change the social order of the United
States. Having lived through those traumatic days, I'm not
going to say that our social order did not require changing;
neither am I going to say we have accomplished a great
deal in moving our society along the road. But I will say
that the question that bothers me most in the whole general
field of social endeavor wasn't even considered forty,
thirty, or even twenty years ago. That question is whether
a new social order in the United States can be sustained
by the efforts of a few industrious citizens. In short, I am
plagued with wondering whether the few can provide for
the many. Now, if we say they can, we are saying that the
money produced by a decreasing percentage of our population is supporting an increasing percentage of the population. If this could happen to any degree, then where is the
breakline? In other words, at what point do we find that
the social order can no longer change solely as the result of
an expenditure of money? Or, if we admit that the social
order has not been changed in geometric proportion or even
in direct proportion to the expenditure of money, when
does the whole structure break down?

If any civilization in the history of the world has ever solved this question, I have never heard of it. And believe me, we are not, by any means, the first civilization that has recognized the problems of the poor, the underprivileged, and the people who are denied the same advantages that others enjoy. This lack is no fault of some of the people affected; but there are those who find themselves on the short end because they are just plain lazy.

The civilizations to which I have referred tried, just as we have tried, to correct these conditions. But they never seemed to succeed. Consequently, would it not be wise for us at this point in our history to take a long, hard look at the successes we have had in changing the social order and, more importantly, at the failures we have experienced? Only then can the right changes be made—if indeed they can be made at all.

This question, then—whether we can change our pursuits so that failures can be avoided—becomes a very important one for those in power in the federal government. Certainly the government must be strong enough to prevent further detrimental actions in this area of fiscal irresponsibility and to produce whatever changes are needed to correct present conditions.

The following illustrates a source of power that very few of us had recognized until recent years. It was brought into very sharp focus early in President Ford's tenure, when he asked that the 5.5 percent automatic cost-of-living pay increases for federal employees be held up for several months to bring about savings of $700 million. At the mere suggestion, civil employees in Washington were up in arms. They added their great power to the power of the bureaucracies they represented and, on the day the vote on the increase was to be taken, filled the halls of Congress, the

Gallery, and every niche in the Capitol where a congressman or a senator could be found. With all these people
looking down their backs, the congressmen, our national
lawmakers, turned down the president's very sensible, logi-
cal request. Therefore, because of civil-employee and bureaucratic power, the president's effort to slow down automatic pay increases proved futile. In fact, civil employees
are now demanding that instead of the 5.5 percent increases,
they be given the full increases to which they feel they are
entitled.

And in a way we can't blame them. They didn't ask
for those automatic pay increases. Congressmen, including
senators, saw some political sex appeal in this approach
and wrote the increases into the law. Those who have been
the beneficiaries of their largesse are not about to allow the
law to be changed.

I think the question boils down to this: Do the Congress
and the Administration have the courage to say No to such
built-in destroyers of monetary security, these built-in
creators and accelerators of inflation? If the courage to say
No is not in these places, then we are saying No to a continuation of our strength which has historically been in our
freedom.

In fact, there doesn't seem to be any evidence of the
courage it takes to stand up to those forces in this country
who are demanding, just as all eventually unsuccessful
civilizations have demanded before, that fewer and fewer
of the people work harder and harder to support more
and more of the people who are not working.

But I'm getting ahead of myself. The problem at the
moment is in understanding how the United States reached
its present position after only two hundred years of existence.

Like all other problems involving government and the people, two considerations are paramount: governmental power and individual freedom. Earlier, I mentioned that the authority of the legislative branch was literally forced on President Franklin Roosevelt in the early years of the 1930s when this nation's people were unhappy, discouraged, and downright fearful of the future. FDR, perhaps more than any other leader the world has ever known, with the possible exception of Winston Churchill, looked and acted like a man who knew the answers, who had all of our problems in hand, and who could lead us out of the economic morass of a depression if only we would supply the tools.

The legislative equipment was already his. The people elected huge majorities in Congress to support him and carry out his legislative programs in the quickest possible time. Immediate, devastating, frightening problems, such as the need to halt banking operations, could not await the time Congress required to debate and hassle over them, so the president was moved into taking unprecedented actions. It is unlikely that any man in American history has ever before been given this kind of power over his fellowmen without even asking for it. But it did happen and President Roosevelt began by using the power wisely and well. But there came a day when the power he wielded was not enough for him. The president of the depression-ridden thirties wanted more power and he wanted it in the one branch that had been able to exercise a check on executive authority—the judiciary. The upshot of all this led to FDR's first major defeat on an issue which went to the people for a decision. Old-timers in politics as well as young students of that era will remember the period I refer to. It was when FDR attempted to "pack" the United States Supreme Court so that more of his questionable recovery legislation would be upheld and welded into the American governmental system. To achieve his aim, Roosevelt took to the hustings and actively worked for the defeat of some powerful Democratic senators who were opposed to his ideas for altering the membership and structure of the Supreme Court.

The shift of power to the executive branch, however, had begun earlier—in the winter of 1933–34. At first the power bills were "short-term," one of the first measures being the Civil Works Administration to provide "temporary" federal jobs for the nation's unemployed. By 1935, though, President Roosevelt had decided on a more permanent program called the Works Progress Administraion.

The arguments FDR and his team of liberal advisors used on behalf of the WPA sound faintly familiar when repeated today. Harry L. Hopkins, then head of the Federal Emergency Relief Administration and a close friend of the president, assured the nation that direct relief—or a dole— maintains life "not at a subsistence level, but at a level of deterioration." He spoke emotionally of the "loss of skill, the loss of work habits, muscle, and resolve," to say nothing of the individual American's loss of his sense of importance to himself and his family—and to society—should the dole become permanent.

In view of what has happened since, perhaps Hopkins' most memorable statement was this: "The most ominous threat which the unemployed can hold over the present structure is that they should as a class be perpetuated, unwillingly unproductive, and held in a straitjacket of idleness."

Hopkins was right, as we now know. For, with the energetic help of social engineers working for the federal bureaucracy, several generations of unemployed have been peopled with the kind of relief recipients he described and who now heavily influence elections. But few government officials or members of Congress thought that this could or would happen at the time, and as a result, the legislation that was to lay the foundation for the welfare state of today zipped through the Congress with huge majorities.

The cornerstone of this legislation was the Social Security Act which FDR began working on in 1933 and which was signed into law on August 14, 1935. In this period New Dealers made much of the argument that, in this area, the United States lagged decades behind the nations of Western Europe in the development of a comprehensive social security program to take care of the nation's aged citizens in their twilight years.

One-time Secretary of Labor Frances Perkins, in her memoirs of the Roosevelt years, described how the program developed gradually from a general idea into specific legislation. She explained that Roosevelt was determined to have a self-maintaining system—one in which all benefits paid out were to be supported by premiums paid in. "But the suffering of those now out of work, or the aged or dependent or sick, for whom no such premium ever could be paid, challenged our immediate attention," Mrs. Perkins wrote.

"We agreed that we must bring in a program for unemployment insurance and one for old-age insurance. Without too much debate we agreed that in addition . . . we must recommend what we knew was not insurance but a relief program. It must include old-age assistance, assistance for dependent children, assistance for the crippled and handicapped persons and a continuation of emergency assistance to the unemployed then in operation."

This, then, was where the groundwork for the welfare

state was actually laid. Now the question is: How many nonworkers can the workers support? We have to know where the line of refusal to support runs in our system. Maybe it runs until it becomes impossible for the workers any longer to handle the job. *We need to know the breakpoint.*

The Social Security system was a forerunner to FDR's ill-fated effort to take over the power wielded by the Supreme Court and it was the presidential election of 1936 that brought the struggle to a head. For the first time in this century, the word "mandate" came into popular usage in connection with contemporary politics.

President Roosevelt had offered the electorate benefits for the jobless and aged as well as help for small businessmen, small farmers, and organized labor. And more than ever he had put the emphasis on "soak-the-rich" taxes. The result was 27,476,673 votes for FDR to 16,676,583 for Alfred ("Alf") M. Landon. In the landslide, FDR had carried every state but Maine and Vermont.

Now Roosevelt began to take seriously the talk of a mandate from the voters. In his inaugural address on January 20, 1937, he rang all the bells of the "haves"-versus-the-"have-nots"-theme and declared the United States was far from reaching the "goal of our vision." When he announced that one-third of the nation was ill-housed, ill-clad, and ill-nourished, he was tacitly saying that these national maladjustments could not be rectified so long as a conservative Supreme Court was invalidating New Deal legislation.

Then, suddenly, in February 1937, he proposed a plan for adding under certain conditions as many as six new justices to the Court. Overnight a violent debate broke out—a nationwide controversy that included the entire

New Deal program and the American constitutional system.

The New Dealers scoffed at charges that they were attempting to pack the Supreme Court. They said the Court had been packed for years in the interests of the "economic Royalists" and the political supporters of big business.

FDR's opponents fought back with unusual force. They called the plan a proposal without precedent designed to subjugate the Court to the will of Congress and the president and to thwart the Constitution.

In an adverse report submitted by the Senate Committee on the Judiciary, filed June 7, 1937, Sen. William H. King (D–Utah) stated:

"Its ultimate operation would be to make this government one of men rather than one of laws and its practical operation would be to make the Constitution what the Executive or Legislative branches of government choose to say it is—an interpretation to be changed with each change of administration.

"It is a measure which should be so emphatically rejected that its parallel will never again be presented to the free representatives of the free people of America."

King echoed the views of many of the opponents of the Court-packing plan when he went on to say that it was the first time in history that a proposal to alter the decisions of the Court by increasing its personnel had been so boldly made.

"Let us now set a salutary precedent that will never be violated," he said. "Let us of the 75th Congress in words that will never be disregarded by any succeeding Congress declare that we would rather have an independent Court, a fearless Court, a Court that will dare to announce its honest opinion in what it believes to be the defense of the liberties of the people, than a Court that, out of fear or a sense of obligation to the appointing power, or factional passion, approves any measure we may enact. We are not judges of the judges. We are not above the Constitution."

President Roosevelt's program was vigorously but unsuccessfully supported by Robert M. La Follette, Jr., a progressive liberal from Wisconsin. He argued that it was not the Constitution but the decisions of the majority of the justices which stood in the way of necessary legislation regarding labor, agriculture, finance, and the conservation of our human and material resources.

"Our Founding Fathers," he said, "never intended the Supreme Court to be the dictator of this nation."

And, I might add, neither did they intend the president to have the same power.

Fortunately President Roosevelt lost the Supreme Court fight and suffered his first major defeat of the New Deal years. But by that time the welfare state was well on its way, and this was more than a program—it was a concept, actually a way of life initiated by the government. Once launched, it could never be anything but a system that would grow larger and larger, cost the taxpayer more and more of his earnings, and make him more and more dependent on fewer and fewer savings.

This was a very crucial period in the history of our nation. It was the time when Uncle Sam moved into social engineering on a broad and very costly scale, and never came out; the time when we were lining up a long series of federal spending deficits that has caused the trouble with which President Ford is currently groping.

This is when Social Security got its start, and when the Congress enacted unemployment compensation, aid to dependent children, and many other programs that appealed to the liberals but still cost just as much of the taxpayer's money. These were the times—in the midst of the Great Depression of the thirties—that actually required many costly attempts to help the needy. Nobody then ever thought these programs would become permanent. But they never stopped. The nation grew larger in terms of population, and the programs grew larger in terms of expense.

Very few people today realize that it was World War II, not the New Deal program, that got us out of the 1930s' depression. Hard as it is to believe, this nation went from an unemployment crisis in 1937 to a manpower shortage in 1940. It happened so fast that few even recognized the change. However, one thing did not, and has not, altered, and that is "welfare." The monster which now threatens to devour us continues to demand and expect the government to finance its every need, regardless of the economic situation existing at the moment. The welfare population has become entirely dependent on government services financed by the industry of others.

Before long the Ford Administration will have to conduct a massive investigation along the lines of the Hoover Commission studies to find out just which programs and agencies are required and just which people are cheating on them, for the world's largest bureaucracy is spawning an ever-increasing number of fraud charges involving federal officials and recipients of government monies. In aggregate the allegations involve billions of dollars; in the welfare system alone, fraud and mismanagement are alleged to run into the hundreds of millions.

Some of the most serious charges have been brought against the federally insured Student Loan Program, administered by the United States Department of Health, Education, and Welfare (HEW). Federal and state officials have begun investigating a long list of these, which include collusion on a nationwide level among federal officials and owners of schools that operate for profit, illegal lending practices of participating banks, and deceptive advertising by some of the schools.

The *Wall Street Journal* quoted a federal law enforcement officer as saying the student loan scandal "is going to be bigger" than the Billy Sol Estes scandal in the 1960s. (Estes was a Texas operator who sold finance companies $24 million worth of mortgages on nonexistent fertilizer tanks.)

The *Journal* further quoted the authorities as saying that the loss to the government could run to $500 million or more. HEW officials claim that stupidity, greed, and inertia "were big factors" in the irregularities now under investigation.

The federal student loan program is eleven years old. In that time it has dispersed loans totaling $8 billion to 4.5 million students. It permits undergraduates to borrow up to $2,500 a year from private lenders at 7 percent interest (an additional 3 percent is currently paid to the lenders by the government). Repayment is insured by the government in case the student defaults on the loan. The program includes more than 8,800 schools and colleges, 1,700 vocational and other schools which operate for profit, and nearly 19,000 lending institutions.

One of the problems has been caused by the folding of several hundred proprietary schools in recent years. Students charge that they are being held liable for the repayment of their federal loans even in cases where the schools closed before the students graduated.

The waste and inefficiency of abusive power in our government are not confined to any one bureau or department, but stretch across the whole sprawling mess we call the federal bureaucracy. In subsequent chapters I shall try to point out other instances of irregularities, abuses, and needless expenditures. I shall start with the bureaucrats because I honestly feel this group has more to do with running the government than any other group in the country.

In the last few years—actually, in the period that began with our grave concern over pollution and the creation of an Environmental Protection Agency (EPA)—more and more Americans have been finding their lives regulated by decrees from Washington. Almost unnoticed, the stream of regulations and dictates has become a genuine flood. Most of them are written by bureaucrats whom no one sees and no one has ever heard of.

According to the *Reader's Digest,* in 1973 the *Federal Register* needed 35,591 pages to publish all the new decrees: in 1974 it required 45,422 pages. And to enforce the new and old decrees spewed out by government bureaus, Uncle Sam maintains an ever-growing army of investigators and informers. Although the Central Intelligence Agency gets most of the publicity, the fact remains that, over and above the 12,000 to 16,000 CIA investigators and the additional thousands who work for military intelligence units, the government has some 60,000 men and women who function as investigators. They are scattered among forty-four separate departments, agencies, and commissions of the federal government.

According to the Civil Service Commission, the exact total is 60,716 as of October 1973. This represents an increase of 16,676 over the 44,040 investigators reported in a similar study in 1964. And the number has undoubtedly increased since the 1973 computation.

The primary reason for the increased number of investigators has been new legislation such as the Civil Rights Act, the Wholesome Meat Act, and the creation of the Environmental Protection Agency as well as other measures requiring enforcement personnel. Following is a computation of the number of investigators and what they are doing:

19,517 investigate criminal activities.

8,045 protect and police public property.

7,081 inspect meat and poultry for purity.

6,306 assess and collect delinquent taxes.

3,864 inspect imported goods.

2,653 enforce equal-rights laws.

2,082 check aviation personnel and equipment.

1,639 patrol U.S. borders.

1,317 check the safety of foods and drugs.

1,234 investigate immigrants arriving in the United States.

1,224 do general investigating, including security clearances.

1,055 inspect coal mines.

699 enforce wage-and-hour laws.

278 inspect imported goods held in bond.

213 check railroad equipment for safety.

186 enforce game laws.

180 supervise food and drug inspections.

175 examine farm-commodity warehouses.

150 investigate aviation accidents.

133 inspect ships arriving at U.S. ports.

103 enforce public-health laws.

38 enforce customs regulations.

2,544 have miscellaneous inspection duties.

III / Red Tape, Waste, and Boondoggles

A mother suffering from brain damage had her government disability and child-support payments delayed ten months because of a computor error in Washington . . . a mother of five children was declared ineligible for benefits from the government through a mistake in a federal bureau . . . an elderly couple had their Social Security benefits cut off for eleven months because the agency involved had misplaced their records. . . .

These are typical of the cases referred to my office as a result of bureaucratic mismanagement on an increasing scale in Washington and elsewhere throughout the country. They come wrapped in the kind of red tape that only government can manufacture.

These are often matters of survival, not politics. They deeply, and perhaps permanently, affect the lives of the people involved. And when I say the people involved, I mean the people who unjustly had their benefits withheld.

One thing that runs through all the cases which come to my office is an element of total confusion and complete governmental indifference. To the army of bureaucrats—federal, state, and local—which now number 14,000,000—7 percent of the population—the claimants represent nothing more than some data punched on a computer card. But it is a different matter when it involves federal government employees and the expenditure of money collected from the American taxpayers for such projects as a study of the blood groups of Polish Zlotnika pigs, for which Uncle Sam put up $20,000. This is one of those studies that falls into a strange category of government projects which may or may not have some strained reason to justify undertaking them.

But while the cases of human distress mentioned at the start of this chapter and this apparent boondoggle project are miles apart in character and worth, they both serve to point up the government's attitude in matters concerning its individual citizens. In the former instances, Uncle Sam made it plain that the government couldn't have cared less whether its Social Security computer was back on the beam and helping Americans dependent upon its proper functioning; or, as far as the Polish pigs were concerned, whether anything actually came of the costly experiments.

No government can afford to become emotionally involved in its bureaucratic projects. This is why only the citizens who foot the bill will ever be able to do anything about projects such as the following:

—A $57,500 study by the University of Pittsburgh on "Community and National Integration" in the People's Republic of China.

—A $20,000-a-year study of German cockroaches by the National Institute of Health.

—A $70,000 project to conduct research on the smell of perspiration from Australian aborigines. This is one of sixteen subprojects concerned with the "zoophysiology" in Alaska. The purpose of the subproject—to learn about man's adaptation to his environment—involved a comparison of the Alaskan Eskimo with the Australian aborigine and their reactions to climate.

—An $8,700 grant awarded by the National Foundation on the Arts and the Humanities for a study of the history of comic books in the nineteenth century. The focus of the project was on the social and political style of comic-strip presentations.

—A payment of $500 to a writer for a poem only seven letters long. The poem (all of it) is as follows: "lighght." It was written by Aram Saroyan, son of author William Saroyan, and was selected for the American Literary Anthology.

—A $46,089 grant to the University of California at Los Angeles for a dictionary of witchcraft entitled *American Popular Beliefs and Superstitions.*

Not only is the idea of a dictionary of witchcraft a ridiculous pursuit to be financed with federal dollars, but it constitutes an unwarranted example of government competition with private industry. Certainly if a great demand exists for such a publication, America has an ample number of publishing houses ready, willing, and eager to meet it. There was no need for the government to step in.

This, of course, is not a full listing of the stupid-sounding projects which show up each year in the federal budget. There is a $19,200 study inaugurated to figure out why kids fall off their tricycles. Others which absolutely raise the hackles on the taxpayer's neck these days are studies of toads in Central America, ants in Indo-Austria, wild boars in Pakistan, lizards in Yugoslavia, catfish in India, and whistling ducks in Texas.

In all fairness, some of these projects suffer from bureaucratic stupidity in the way they are described. Some, according to the General Accounting Office (GAO), have a sound basis for their existence in the budget. Others, however, are little bits and pieces pulled together by federal bureaucrats in their efforts to build a personal empire before Uncle Sam gets around to discovering that they are not doing much to justify their existence on the federal payroll.

Throughout the years, American taxpayers have simmered under the collar at this kind of waste. If that was their reaction in years when the economy was healthy, what must it be today, especially if they happen to be among the unemployed?

For example, just try selling an unemployed steelworker on the idea that the government needs tax money to put out a dictionary on witchcraft and you'll get a genuine earful of what the economic situation is all about. Other American taxpayers today are even more expressive. They claim they are being "ripped off" by the bureaucrats who are out to find ways and means to spend *their* money.

If the senseless nature of many boondoggle projects is inclined to infuriate the American taxpayer, he would really be up in arms if he knew the actual reason behind these awards, grants, and handouts, which is this: The existence of many of these far-out projects is a drive on the part of federal bureaucrats to spend before the end of each fiscal year on June 30 all the money voted them by Congress. Mike Causey, a columnist for the *Washington Post*, has kept a close eye on this phenomenon for many years. In the June 16, 1975 edition of the paper he wrote his annual column about what he calls the "spend-it-or-lose-it-derby." Here is the way he describes it:

. . . With only 14 days left to participate, some agencies are unloading money with the same zeal as shut-ins sent to a summer clearance sale with a fistful of disappearing dollars.

July 1 is the start of a new fiscal year, and many federal offices are disposing of leftover money for travel, office furniture, or just about anything else they can think of.

Under the sometimes cockeyed federal budget system, agencies found guilty·of not spending all they have by midnight June 30 will be forced to suffer the humiliation of returning it to the Treasury.

Those agencies know, too, that they will have to face the grilling of congressional committees that will demand to know why the agencies asked for more money than was needed. So the simplest way to keep everybody happy and stay out of trouble, some believe, is to buy everything in sight until the money is gone.

The mad June spending splurge, which began last month in some farsighted federal offices, is not necessarily the mindless buying binge it appears to the untrained federal observer. On the other hand, sometimes it is precisely that.

An example of the bad came a few years ago. One executive branch agency discovered, to its horror, that pots of money were left over with July 1 staring the agency in the face. Rather than suffer the slings and arrows of hard-eyed Treasury auditors and congressional budget bulldogs, the agency took the easy way out.

It ordered, paid for and had installed—all before the June 30 deadline—a batch of fancy and very, very expensive oak doors for the offices of its bigwigs. Previously, the officials had nice doors on their inner sanctums but not the rich oak slammers which remain to this day the envy of other departments. . . .

The spend-it-or-lose-it system is partly the fault of congressional committees, who provide funds in the name of the taxpayers, and the government's short-range 12-month budgeting cycle. . . .

Public disgust over this high-handed extravagance is fortunately becoming more and more vocal.

The National Science Foundation, for example, has recently come under strong criticism from Sen. William Proxmire for wasting the taxpayers' money on questionable social science research projects such as:

—A $132,500 University of Minnesota study to determine why people fall in love.

—A $342,000 Michigan State University study on the use of birth control devices by unmarried college students. The study questioned 1,200 students as to when, where, and with whom they had premarital sex.

—A $350,000 study on nonconformity which found that 48 percent of the American people believe in the Devil.

—A study to determine how to integrate hitch-hiking into the transportation system.

While Administration officials preach economy, hundreds of White House employees avail themselves of free picture-framing services that cost the taxpayers $92,000 each year.

While the Urban Mass Transportation Administration (UMTA) urges Americans to use public transportation, it provides its employees with indoor subsidized parking at $6 per month as compared with local commercial rates of $45 per month.

While the White House urges Americans to conserve gasoline, eight hundred federal officials are chauffered around the capital in limousines.

John Stender, former assistant secretary of labor for Occupational Safety and Health, spent seventy days last year traveling on "official business" to Nevada, Florida, Puerto Rico, and Hawaii, plus seven trips to his home state of Washington. Stender told the *Wall Street Journal* that every trip he makes is at the invitation of some group with a "deep interest" in occupational safety and health.

The government maintains two plush resorts for the sole use of high federal officials, members of Congress, and civilian VIPs. One is in Virginia's Shenandoah National Park; the other, a lakeside mansion, is in Grand Teton National Park in Wyoming. Walter Cronkite and his family were recent guests at one of these taxpayer-supported resorts.

Rep. Robert Drinan (D–Mass.) recently had his entire 1974 voting record printed in the *Congressional Record* for "informational purposes." The cost for the twenty-two-page record: $5,720. If each member of Congress had his voting record printed in the *Record* each year using as many pages as Drinan, it would cost the taxpayers over $3 million annually. In addition to giving themselves free printing privileges, members of Congress retain the right to *change* their actual remarks in the *Record*. Therefore the *Record* paid for by the taxpayer is not a record at all, but merely a representation of what the Congress wants the public to know about an actual debate and discussion.

For instance, a legislator's aide can walk into the *Record*'s office, ask the reporter for a copy of everything his boss has said that day, sit at a table provided especially for the purpose, and go through the copy, line by line, cutting or embellishing the legislator's remarks as much as he wishes. Another example of the liberties taken with the *Record* is the all-too-typical incident that occurred on May 12, 1975, the day the Senate took up the NASA Authorization Bill providing for the fiscal year 1976 program of the National Aeronautics and Space Administration. It was my duty, as the ranking minority member of the Senate Committee on Aeronautical and Space Sciences, to be present on the Senate floor at all times during consideration of that measure and to assist the chairman in defending the committee's bill. When proceedings on the measure closed without any amendments being proposed or any speeches being made in opposition to it, I thought the published debate would accurately reflect these facts.

It does not. Using a privilege conferred on each senator

by no more authority than a letter of the Joint Senate Leadership, a senator who was not present at any time during the debate on the NASA budget inserted a speech attacking the bill. This opposing speech is prominently placed in the *Record* as though it had been given during the Senate deliberations. Anyone who had not been in the chamber at the time of the debate would get the impression, from reading the *Record,* that the managers of the committee bill had rudely ignored the opposing senator or had not had the answers with which to reply to him.

The Equal Employment Opportunity Commission had a case backlog of 100,000 complaints and had illegally spent $800,000 before it finally came under fire from Congress, which forced the commission to suspend three high officials for twenty days without pay, and demanded that henceforth the GAO audit the EEOC accounts.

There is a national commission on gambling, set up by a 1970 law. The commission's goal is a 1979 report to determine how widespread gambling really is and what rules the federal government should make concerning it. The commission seeks to conduct surveys to find out how many Americans bet, how much they bet, how many are compulsive gamblers, and so forth.

The House Appropriations Subcommittee on Labor-HEW overwhelmingly rejected a proposed budget recision of $291.7 million in Hill-Burton funds—which subsidize the construction of hospitals—even though the director of the Hill-Burton project testified that there is an excess of hospital beds in most areas of the country.

The Federal Home Loan Bank Board recently bought three color television cameras to film the news conferences of its chairman. The films will be sent to twelve district home loan banks.

Why all the interest in government spending on "social programs"? Because by 1980 an estimated 40 percent of the national income will be spent on knowledge-related activities compared with just 25 percent for manufacturing.

From Kevin Phillips' book, *Mediacracy:**

—In 1948 the federal government spent $1 billion for research and development; in 1974 it spent $20 billion.

—In 1940 national expenditures for education were $3.2 billion; in 1973 they were $96 billion.

—In 1953 HEW spent about $2 billion; in 1972 it spent $52 billion.

—Between 1940 and 1973 the number of tax-exempt foundations rose from 314 to 28,000, with combined assets of more than $20 billion.

Sen. John McClellan (D–Ark.), chairman of the Senate Appropriations Committee, has pointed out that federal outlays for social programs—education, manpower, health, and income maintenance—have more than tripled in the last *ten* years from $79 billion to $255 billion.

One of the major effects of the greatly expanded federal spending programs has been to attract more special-interest groups to the nation's capital. Indeed, almost overnight, Washington has become the mecca for a new breed of lobbyist. The latest army of special pleaders differs from the old-time lobbyist who registers with the Department of Justice and goes to work to influence the course of legislation. The latest arrivals are interested primarily in influencing government agencies and bureaucrats who, through the power of regulation, are more important to some businesses than new laws.

There is no way to estimate the number of corpora-

---

*New York, Doubleday, 1975.

tions, universities, foundations, and institutes that have in recent years opened offices in Washington to track down contracts, grants, and assistance money available from the national government. Only six years ago Washington trailed several other large cities in the number of trade and professional associations located within its boundaries. However, the Metropolitan Board of Trade recently disclosed that the number of such groups has tripled since 1969. As a result, Washington now is ahead of New York City and all other areas in the association business.

Other special-interest groups depend on influential law firms to make sure they don't get short-changed by bureaucrats who have ready access to the federal treasury. Many of these firms are heavily staffed with lawyers who formerly worked for regulatory agencies such as the Security and Exchange Commission, the Federal Trade Commission, and the Federal Communications Commission, to name but a few. The growing power and influence of this private legal community was the subject of a recent series of articles in the *Washington Star*.

Despite attempts by the Ford Administration to curb the authority of the regulatory agencies, they are gaining more power every day. The intent of Congress, and many times the intent of the Administration, is often lost in the maze of governmental superstructures so huge that only trained experts with years of experience can find their way around in them. But while the Administration—until now—has proven almost helpless, the people are beginning to put at least a partial rein on the power of these bureaucracies. More and more legal actions are being brought against federal agencies which have ignored or refused to abide by new laws adopted by Congress. A report last summer in the *Washington Post* stated: "Court actions against federal agencies are becoming common; Congress passes a law, an agency ignores it, the people sue and the court acts. . . ."

An example of the type of legal action that is becoming more frequent is a recent suit brought by seventeen farm-worker organizations against the Department of Labor for not taking action to assist migrant farm workers in accordance with the law. The outcome was that Judge Charles B. Richey of the U.S. District Court in Washington ordered the Department of Labor to deliver "all manpower services, benefits and protections, including the full range of counseling, testing, training, and job referral services authorized by law" to the migrant workers, in compliance with the Wagner-Peyser Act, which affects an estimated five million workers and their dependents in the migrant field.

In effect the court challenged the Washington bureaucracy and the officials in 50 state employment-service programs and 2,700 field offices to abide by the federal statutes.

The news that the American people are at long last beginning to take matters into their own hands to curb the excesses and arrogance of the federal power brokers is encouraging. It has long been my belief that the only way we can make any progress against bureaucratic power is by the American people becoming sufficiently aroused to demand changes.

IV / Who Runs the
Government?

Who actually runs the government?

I can tell you for certain it is not the president of the
United States, nor his cabinet, nor the Congress. It is the
army of government bureaucrats in Washington and across
the nation who hold the kind of power it takes to complicate the lives of American citizens and destroy the freedoms
which the Founding Fathers intended them to have.

When I consider the problem of the enormous bureaucracy in this country, I am reminded of the first time I
talked with President Nixon after his election in 1968. I
told him that if he didn't get control of the federal bureaucracy within six months, he would never control his Administration.

Although he did not say so, I got the distinct impression that the president thought I was overstating the case
of how powerful the "middle management" bureaucracy
is in the federal government. Possibly he might have recalled our conversation a year or two later when his Administration began to "leak like a sieve." Regardless, a
point was reached when every move the president and his
team had taken in secret or contemplated in private wound
up in the news columns of *The New York Times*, the
Washington Post, and various other politically unfriendly
segments of the news media. Even relatively unimportant

conferences, such as some that I attended in the White House, were reported with astounding accuracy in Jack Anderson's column. One in particular not only quoted what every person in the president's Oval Office had said, but even had the sequence of the statements correctly reported.

This situation, which was more serious than most Nixon critics have admitted, is what led to the ill-advised creation of the White House "plumbers" unit and other actions that smacked of a fit of official paranoia where the news media were concerned. In fairness, I can see how a steady buildup of leaks to the press would alarm a president. However, I can't for the life of me understand how a president or anyone else representing the federal government could sanction illegal operations such as burglary. This is especially true in a time when widespread crime had become such a problem that its eradication was a major political promise of the men who created the plumbers unit and directed its activities.

President Nixon must have known that secrecy was possible if proper measures were taken. One prime example was the Kissinger mission to Peking, which set the stage for the president's personal visit to Communist China. Not a breath of that operation leaked, even though it was a story that contained one of the highest news quotients of all time.

I learned of the projected visit while flying in a jet over Oklahoma City: Fort Worth Center radioed me that the White House had been trying to reach me. They patched me in to the White House and Dr. Kissinger got on, said an announcement on his trip to Peking would be made about the time I landed, and asked that I not mention it to anyone.

But this was an exception. Most important announcements are leaked by entrenched bureaucrats who wield an almost unbelievable brand of power that is hidden and practically unlimited. Year after year they make hash of presidential as well as congressional intent. As a result, today we find American lives almost totally ruled by bureaucratic decisions, regulations, and opinions that are all too often arbitrary, capricious, or uninformed.

The tremendous size of the federal government was a major concern of mine when I was first elected to the Senate over twenty years ago. As some of you will recall, it was a time when we heard much discussion about big government; the interrelationship of government agencies on the federal, state, and local level; and the need for an equitable distribution of revenue sources among these divisions. It was also a time when the Hoover Commission was making a determined attempt to catalogue the federal government's various activities and functions and making recommendations to end some of the incredible program duplication, overlapping functions, and inefficient and wasteful administrative practices it found. I do not plan here to go into the sound and constructive recommendations made by the Hoover Commission which were never acted upon or even given consideration. It is enough to recall that in terms of money and efficiency enormous dividends were realized from the recommendations which *were* implemented.

But all that was years ago and since that time—especially over the last decade—the size of the federal establishment has grown tremendously. In fact, the bureaucracy which dominates the federal government today has actually become a problem of man's ability to govern himself in a time of tremendous technological change and population growth. It is so massive that it literally feeds on itself, so intricate that it lends itself to a wide range of abuses, some criminal and deliberate, others unwitting and inept. It is so large that no one in or out of government can accurately define its power and scope, and institutions doing business with it, or attempting to do business with it, are forced to hire trained experts just to show them through the labyrinth made up of hundreds of departments, bureaus, commissions, offices, and agencies. Some colleges and universities, for example, employ specialists called "grant finders," whose job it is to inform these schools what is available to them under the various laws and multitudinous regulations of the federal establishment.

Every now and then we catch a frightening glimpse of this enormous structure and what it means in terms of accountability and manageability. For example, a young member of the House of Representatives several years ago set out to determine how many assistance programs were maintained by the federal government. It took him two years to find out that there were over 1,300, many of which were unknown to each other, unknown to anyone within the government itself, and unknown to the people they were established to help.

As a result of these findings, in 1969 Congressman, now Senator, William D. Roth, Jr., of Delaware, published his own catalogue of the government's assistance programs in a book entitled *A Listing of Operating Federal Assistance Programs Compiled During the Roth Study.* In 1972 the Government Printing Office took over the job with a *Catalogue of Federal Domestic Assistance.*

Then we had the spectacle several years ago of the House of Representatives engaging in a tense, prolonged, and emotional battle over the appropriation of funds for

rat control in our major cities. After all the shouting had
died down, it was discovered that *eight* programs already
existed in various government departments for the purpose
of doing the same thing!

The size of the federal bureaucracy—which, like Topsy,
just keeps growing year after year despite the unfair and
growing burden it places on the taxpayer—is compounding
the difficulty and confusion that the average American en-
counters as he attempts to function in today's society. If
this continues, the day will come when not only will
business choke to death on government red tape, but the
average American wage earner and property holder will
suffocate under the centralized power that our founders
made such efforts to prevent.

Amazingly, this problem, for all its size, complexity, and
importance, does not seem to be receiving the kind of
study and attention that should be accorded it by today's
leaders. Occasionally a former member of that vast bureaucracy attempts to explain what is going on. One of these is
Mr. Lee Loevinger, a Washington attorney previously with
the Federal Communications Commission. In an article he
wrote for the magazine *The Business Lawyer,* Mr. Loevinger warned that the greatest danger stemming from the
problem of bureaucracy is not that of error but of ignor-
ance. He explained:

If man is to have any hope of finding a path to a livable
future, he must first take a clear-eyed look at this present
situation and the institutions of his creation which surround
and influence him. The most persuasive social institution of
the modern age, the most characteristic social problem of the
exponential growth of recent years, is bureaucracy. It is like a
passionless mob which can capture and conquer man unless
he is wise enough to subdue it and shape it to his own pur-

poses. This can be done, but first we must study its nature and its laws, and recognize that, for the contemporary world, bureaucracy is not an answer to our problems but is itself one of the principal problems that is both a part and a product of exponential growth that modern society must learn to understand and control.

Mr. Loevinger's conclusion is correct. Before we can understand and control the federal bureaucracy, we will have to get an adequate look at it. We have not had anything like an overall view of this enormous entity since the Hoover Commission reports, and very frankly, I am beginning to have some doubts as to whether such a study could be undertaken in time to yield maximum benefits. It took William Roth and his investigators two years to come anywhere close to an accurate picture of just how many assistance programs exist in the government. Considering the vast, sprawling reach of the federal bureaucracy into every facet of American life and into every political and governmental subdivision of the fifty states of the Union, it would not surprise me if the listing, explaining, and cataloguing of the various functions and services of a department—such as the Department of Health, Education, and Welfare, for example—took a sizable staff of highly skilled experts five to ten years to do well.

I've already mentioned the evils inherent in this gargantuan monstrosity, which by its very nature lends itself to every kind of abuse. I've also spoken of how its intricacies play into the hands of people skilled in the manipulation of such matters. Now I want to emphasize how this bureaucracy problem thwarts the work in which we in the Senate and the members of the House are engaged. It should not, but probably would, astound most members of the Senate to find out what actually happens to the intent we write into major legislation when it gets into the hands of the bureaucrats. Much of our purpose in enacting laws has been either contradicted, overruled, diluted, or denied in many instances by quasi-judicial rulings by government regulatory agencies, federal enforcement policies, or by the courts. We seem almost complacent in our belief that (1) the people who handle the provisions of the laws we pass will understand the motivation and the intent of the Congress which passed them, and (2) where this intent *is* understood it will be followed without question. I think we all have seen enough examples to realize how far from the actual intent of Congress government bureaucrats have strayed in the administration of the laws —either by design or mistake.

For example, take our latest government program, the Environmental Protection Agency, which was instituted in 1970. The bureaucrats in this agency are interested in clean air, pure water, and so on. I wish them the greatest luck in their current and future endeavors, for there can be no doubt that the American people have misused their most precious heritage, nature, and pollution is becoming a problem of monumental proportions. I believe there was a need for the Environmental Protection Agency and the Clean Air Act it was given to enforce. But having been there when the original proposals were debated and voted upon, I can assure you that the people operating EPA are going far beyond the intent of either the Congress or the president in the way they have started to implement their responsibilities. Never for one second was it considered that the EPA should control land use throughout the nation and direct the future growth of communities already in existence. Yet this is exactly what it is doing in many areas of the country that attract large crowds in cars which, in turn, have an effect upon the atmosphere.

Complaints about EPA's regulations and directives are beginning to flood the Administration from all parts of the country. The complainants stress that while they want clean air and will go to great extremes to guarantee it, they nevertheless want it understood that they did not surrender all their planning authority to the Washington bureaucrats when the EPA bill was actually signed. As one Texas official put it, "When you tell people where they can build parking lots, sports stadiums, and housing complexes, you are controlling the land use." In many parts of the country representatives of the construction industry argue that EPA regulations will destroy them. On the other hand, the Clean Air officials argue that unless their regulations are followed, there will be no responsible urban planning; we'll have nothing but an urban sprawl and a continuing dependence upon pollution-producing automobiles.

Regardless of the end results, we have here a situation where Congress enacts a law to protect the environment and a collection of bureaucrats who were never elected to any kind of official post take that law and interpret it in a way that can make them virtual czars over large segments of the nation's economy. For my part, I don't give a damn whether in some future year an urban sprawl and a continued dependence upon automobiles develop. But right here and now I do give a damn whether the laws I helped to enact are carried out according to legislative intention, which, supposedly, is what the American people wanted, if our form of a democratic republic means anything.

According to legislative intentions, the EPA was created to promote cleaner air and water and to protect the environment in all feasible and reasonable ways. It was *not* set up for the purpose of telling the American people what they could or could not do according to the agency's self-made standards.

Nor was EPA, with or without the help of Ralph Nader, created to build automobiles. Nonetheless, for years EPA has been around with its "made-in-Washington" blueprints for the carmakers in Detroit. When they met resistance, the regulators finally rested their case on an attempt to force U.S. automakers to adopt "catalytic converters" for all new cars, on EPA's assurance that this was the way to reduce exhaust emissions. Detroit finally got tired of the argument and equipped about 85 percent of the 1975 cars with the controversial converters which, incidentally, raised the price of a car by approximately $320. Skeptics who pointed to flaws in the new device were quickly overridden because of the "heat" from Washington and because EPA officials were far from receptive to criticism of any kind. They insisted that the catalytic converters had to be "standard equipment" on all 1975 automobiles. Detroit went ahead when even their pleas for slowing down the schedule were rejected.

The environmentalists had the power in this instance and they used it all. They overpowered not only the automobile industry, but also independent authorities such as the National Academy of Sciences, which also warned against rushing full speed ahead on the converter program.

But EPA won—and then the fun began. All the problems predicted by the skeptics developed, as well as some problems they hadn't even thought of. It almost seemed as though the converter had been waiting to be installed in a car just to show how much trouble it could really cause.

In all events, the carmakers that met EPA's deadline soon learned that leaded gasolines damage the converter's mechanism. They also learned—and this was the clincher—that the converters emitted sulphate mists, which are potentially more harmful to human health than the exhaust emissions they were supposed to prevent.

Only now, as this is written, have the EPA bureaucrats admitted that they bought a "lemon" when they began promoting the converter as a prime antipollution device. Russell Train, director of the EPA, didn't say it that way (bureaucrats never admit costly errors); rather, he announced that EPA was relaxing and revising its emission standards, so the converters won't be needed on 1976 model cars. Not a word was said about the sulfuric acid emissions produced by the converters that made wide-scale use too dangerous even to contemplate.

There is no way to estimate the cost of this goof-up on the part of the EPA regulators. Some people figure it runs into billions of dollars. But one thing is absolutely certain —the cost to the depressed automobile industry has been troublesome and heavy.

This is one of the latest and perhaps one of the most telling examples of the way Uncle Sam can louse up an entire industry with its Big-Brother-knows-best approach to solving the nation's problems. The EPA's obsession with the installation of catalytic converters should serve as a warning to Congress to act cautiously toward any other such proposed measures that could create even more bureaucratic monstrosities. We have enough economic problems at present. What we don't need is another bureaucracy like the EPA, which has an affinity for stupid decisions that cost the taxpayers hundreds of millions of dollars. Let me say again right here that the Congress has already given away too much power to groups and bureaus that do not know how to use it.

This whole business of the intent of Congress being thwarted, nullified, or changed by a group of nameless, faceless bureaucrats has gone on too long and has caused too much trouble. What makes these people believe they know so much more than the men who devise and enact the laws? I'll tell you exactly what it is. These men and women are suffering from "tenuritis," by which I mean they have, because of Civil Service, held the same government jobs for so long that they feel the jobs are part of their personal property and can only be run according to their own personal ideas.

The obstinacy and stubbornness of bureaus that have been too long controlled by men of all major political persuasions proves to me the truth of Lord Acton's famous aphorism: "Power tends to corrupt; absolute power corrupts absolutely." To my mind the power possessed and exercised by the bureaucrats in Washington represents the most dangerous situation in America. If the wrong man should come along and be elected president, we could see a dictatorship erected almost overnight, and it would stem from the loss of power resulting from Congress' failure to live up to its responsibilities. Because the power held in these bureaucratic agencies is power given to them by the Congress which—and I must tell it like it is—was just too damned lazy to take on the job itself.

At this point, let me say that I am not suggesting a return to what was once called the spoils system, in which an incoming national administration cleaned house of all government workers who were not aligned with the new regime's political party. I recognize that this cannot be done, nor should it be done. I further admit that a strong case can be made for the career employee in government and for his protection under the Civil Service system. But I do not agree that this person, blanketed under Civil Service, has an automatic, providential right to permanent employment. Nor do I believe that Civil Service status should empower a civil servant with the right to make his own policy. I believe instead that government employees have a responsibility to the people, who are taxed to pay their salaries, to support and implement the policies that come down to them from the people's elected representatives.

Let me give an example. What do you think would happen in a private corporation if three hundred of its employees held a mass meeting to protest the kind of product their employer was manufacturing? You guessed it. In private industry this kind of effrontery from people whose job is not product design would be rewarded with dismissal notices. Yet several hundred employees of the Department of HEW—none of whom was elected by the people who pay them—held a mass meeting in 1970 to protest policy decisions reached by the White House, the secretary of HEW, and others whose job it is to formulate policy in accordance with the wishes of the people who elected the Administration they serve. And what followed the protesters' actions besides the disruption of HEW's administrative processes and the annoyance of the man chosen by the president to run that department? Nothing. No action was taken at the executive level, nor was a word said in reprimand. This is what it means to hold the kind of power the Washington bureaucracy exercises today.

Understand, I have no objections to any government worker expressing in the proper forum his feeling or belief about any policy. I object most strenuously, however, to the practice of an official using his position as a government employee to undermine, or refuse to work for, the policy of that government.

On the other hand, I don't want to be unfair to career employees in the federal government. The feeling of "ownership" which I detect in their attitudes has come about through long years of bureaucratic possessiveness, and is both a help and a hindrance to the government's efficient administration. In considering this problem, it must be understood that government workers are motivated by much the same considerations as workers in private industry. They are interested in proper compensation and working conditions, and security in both. They oppose change out of fear that it constitutes a threat to their jobs. Therefore their individual and collective efforts, while often derided and criticized as bureaucratic "empire building," are quite understandable.

At the same time, personal ambition, which bears little relationship to efficiency and prudence in the conduct of government business, prompts their attempts to run things to suit their own policy ideas. It is true that bureaucrats and career employees have a great facility for cloaking their actions and projects in terms that sound as though they would improve the efficiency or output of the agencies in which they are employed. But this is very rarely the case. So the whole problem of government employees working their own will on the intent of Congress and on the actual policy of their own administrators results from the long years of permissiveness accorded the middle-management level of government work.

What is more, their refusal to accept innovations and changes in the conduct and method of government business will continue for as long as the federal government's present approach to management is maintained.

But I want to point out right here that this rigid, long-entrenched system, deeply dedicated to its own concept of what is right and what is wrong in the realm of government policymaking, is a denial of the democratic process. I have already mentioned that the system very often nullifies the expressed intent of Congress. Now I want to show how it also thwarts the will of the people.

Ask yourself the following: Why do governments change? Why do we have new administrations? Why do we occasionally see a switch in political affiliations of national administrations? There is one answer to these questions: The changes occur to reflect the will of the qualified voters of the United States.

When the people of this country become dissatisfied with the kind of government they are receiving, they go to the polls and vote to oust the officials responsible. In the old days in the United States, they had a battle cry which reformers used to defeat entrenched and unpopular officials and administrations—"Throw the rascals out." And this is pretty much what happened throughout the history of American politics. When governments change and there is a massive turnover in administrations, it's because the people are voting against the "ins" rather than for those attempting to replace them. There have been exceptions— most notably when the political party opposing the incumbent party fields a national war hero as a candidate. The year 1952 and the election of Gen. Dwight Eisenhower over the nominee of the long-entrenched Democratic party is a case in point.

So we have the will of the people being expressed in the election of new administrations. We have the concern of the people reflected in the elections of new officeholders, new policymakers. But the question is whether the people's will, the people's concern, the people's officially stamped request for a change in direction can ever be completely realized under the present system of bureaucratic management. *I do not think that it can be.* I do not think that the will of the people and the intent of Congress go deep enough into the places where most of the policies directly affecting the people are made. Given the intricacies of the system, the attitude of those in permanent positions, and the general confusion surrounding any change of command in an enterprise as vast as the federal government, I do not think it is possible for this job to be done with any degree of success. The officials oriented to the philosophies promoted by the Democratic party have been in control too long, their numbers are too great, and their influence too strong to bring about within a short time any substantial change in the governmental matters that cause our people so much concern.

I can assure the reader—and this can be attested to by any member of Congress who keeps an accurate count of the mail he receives from his constituents from week to week—that this concern among our people has increased tremendously in the past few years, and it became evident long before Watergate. My office mail, though about average for a senator from a state the size of Arizona, was extremely light when I first came to the Senate in 1953. Of course, it increased enormously prior to 1964, largely because of my nomination as the Republican presidential candidate. But even allowing for Arizona's growth in population and for my status as a one-time candidate for president, my office mail today is at least three times heavier than it was during the fifties, and it reflects a greatly increased concern for America on the part of the people of my state.

The same is true of visitors. Since Arizona is some 2,200 miles away from Washington, my office in the nation's capital does not receive as many visits from constituents as would the office of a member from nearby New York, Ohio,

Pennsylvania, or Virginia. But I am deeply impressed and disturbed at the number of Arizonans who now come to clear up, not only their personal problems connected with the state, but also those having to do with the federal government and its relation to Arizona's communities, land, schools, and hospitals. Each month I get perhaps ten times as many Arizona visitors as I did back in the middle and late 1950s, and possibly three times the number that came in the early sixties.

And Arizonans are certainly not unique in their concern. The uneasiness of all the American people over the problems of government has been steadily and visibly mounting. Therefore, the need for reasonable control of the federal bureaucracy is growing more imperative.

Yet no presidential candidate can honestly promise that he will, if elected, make the changes called for—because he can't do much of anything unless the bureaus say Yes. And the entrenched bureaucrats resist change. They have little or nothing to gain by reform, revision, or innovation. The career executives in charge of the management level of government have learned through long experience to lean and shift with policy-change suggestions coming down from the top, and so they make the absolute minimum number of concessions or none at all to policy pronouncements by cabinet members and bureau chiefs. They know that fundamental changes in policy take a long time to implement and consequently may not have to be completed before a new change at the top occurs. Their attitude is much the same toward policy changes decreed by an act of Congress or even thought of by that body.

To repeat, what we are dealing with here is an administrative maze so complex that many newly appointed policy-making officials spend almost their entire term of office trying to find out precisely what their duties, responsibilities, and functions are. The system lends itself to all kinds of abuse but its major drawback is its enormous, unfathomable size. New cabinet members are often criticized for not having a firmer grasp of the problems relating to their agencies. Very seldom do the critics stop to realize that a mere presidential appointment does not make an administrative expert.

The problem of this enormous and unwieldy bureaucracy is one to which I have devoted endless time and study since 1964, when I became the presidential nominee of the Republican party. I could not afford to run the risk of assuming that Dr. Gallup and his cohorts might not be wrong (as their counterparts in Britain later proved to be in 1974), so I gave long thought and concentrated study to the subject of the structuring, functioning, and staffing of the federal government. The whole matter is so vast that no man with even an outside chance of becoming president can do any less.

When faced with the possibility of occupying the highest office in the land, one begins to understand just how much searching and investigating are necessary merely to find qualified people to fill the top echelons of government. I doubt if the average American has any idea of what a mammoth undertaking this becomes. New presidents literally have to organize teams of trusted friends and associates to conduct wide-range talent hunts, for almost every appointment requires unusual skills. For example, a man who is named to head the Department of Health, Education, and Welfare has to be much more than simply a person with a warm-hearted concern for the needy, the sick, and the undereducated; he has to be an expert in many fields because he will be called upon to act in any number of primary and related fields of social welfare and education and to justify that action before the committees of Congress. And it is commonly believed that all that is needed to head the departments of Commerce and Labor is a good businessman for the former and, for the latter, someone who has had experience with labor contracts and employee disputes. But over the years these departments have grown beyond the confines of their names, and the old, easy assumptions no longer hold. I sometimes think that many politicians and commentators are so uninformed about the complexities of government today that they actually believe aspirants for the job of postmaster general should be rated on the amount of mail they have received.

This subject is so involved that it would take many hours, even days, to do it justice. What I have tried to do here is to detail some of the threatening aspects of the federal bureaucracy and to suggest that it is time to consider new approaches and fresh attitudes in our consideration of how to reduce its power and make it more responsive to the needs of the American people and freedom.

Candor compels me, however, to acknowledge that a large—perhaps the largest—part of this responsibility lies with the legislative branch of the government, at least in the initial phase. In fact, in the area of what government experts refer to as "the principle of accountability," the Congress has simply lost control over most of the money expended by the Treasury each year.

Originally, the Constitution gave Congress control of the nation's purse strings, and Congress designated appropriations committees to act as their agents. But new means of funding have been established which remove control of the appropriations process, not only from the appropriations committees, but from the Congress itself.

And again I stress that this control has been lost to men who were not elected and who are not directly responsible to the people. They are the "gnomes" of Washington. (For those unacquainted with this word: In economic conversations, when referring to the enormous amounts of secret money which have been deposited in numbered accounts with Swiss banks, it is often remarked that the assets of our international financial dealings are controlled by the "gnomes of Zurich.") They cannot be voted out of office if they make costly mistakes, yet they manage the offices in thousands of government buildings, and buy, sell, lend, and borrow assets; manipulate credit, pools, funds, contracts; oversee obligations, debts, accounts; have the authorization to spend from debt receipts and to fix payments and rates. And so on and so on.

Action must be taken if we are to cope with our governmental Frankenstein—the overpowering bureaucracy—and study, investigation, and reorganization all have their parts to play in coming to grips with the problem. Yet I believe that much of the solution lies in selecting the right people for the right jobs, and in making better use of the capabilities and skills of those presently employed in the various government departments. There can be no doubt that people are the key to the success of any enterprise, government or otherwise, especially the ones serving in top-management positions, and I think we have placed too much emphasis on the selection of people who have become recognized and established as experts in a particular field.

It never seems to occur to the people running the government that one way to assure an overbalanced policy in any department is to populate it with employees who are highly experienced in the general area of the department's concern but who have always been aligned with one of several competing viewpoints. This is no way to effect change or innovation. Changes or innovations come about only through people with imagination who are not committed by past experience to the established way of doing business.

It stands to reason that a man who has succeeded in doing things in a given field in a particular, classic way is not going to advocate a new approach. Even if he does—say, on the orders of his immediate superior—he will have no heart for the endeavor and will not push it with the kind of force and determination required.

The dossiers of these middle-management people show that most of them are academicians with impressive degrees. However, this does not mean they possess the know-how and savvy required to do the job well. Sometimes I think our entire government is mesmerized by people holding academic degrees; consequently, people with practical experience and abilities, the ones who could bring fresh ideas to their work, are bypassed when the various posts are filled.

I am fully aware that it is all too easy for those of us who do not have direct responsibility to assign blame and hand out rhetorical prescriptions as to what should be done to improve departmental performances. I know it is a problem which is not going to be corrected overnight. Nor is it one which easily lends itself to any pat solution. I do, however, believe there is great need at the present time for the enlistment of men and women with experience in overall planning techniques. Sometimes they are called "generalists" and described as people who "understand something about everything but not everything about something." As a class, these are people who not only have imagination and experience in general planning and analysis, but who also are more interested in innovation and problem-solving than in the perpetuation of their jobs or in the impact of their views on the formulation of policy.

As I have been trying to point out, the problem of the entrenched bureaucracy is constantly growing. Very soon it may become necessary for the executive branch to attempt some new, almost revolutionary approaches to curtail bureaucratic power and thus reduce the erosion of responsibility for carrying out the will of the people. One proposal is that every few years a number of middle-management employees above a certain government classification be rotated to comparable jobs at the same pay in other government agencies. Now while exchanging X number of persons in grade GS-15 and above from one department with a like number from another department sounds easy enough, it could, in fact, be an administrative impossibility at present. Yet I believe the basic idea is sound even if the method for implementing it has yet to be devised, because it would give the career government employee, especially the one in the middle-management classification, a broader point of view. If he is allowed to spend his entire career in one agency, he is unlikely ever to have the proper appreciation of problems arising in other parts of the government —problems that are often related to his own field of activity. To repeat, I think we need more capable, well-informed generalists and fewer specialists who are so dedicated to one point of view that they are afflicted with what government officials call "tunnel vision." We also need better managers in all departments and bureaus.

There are many ways in which this enormous bureaucratic problem can be tackled. I personally am not wedded to any particular stratagem or method, but I do believe very strongly that the time is long past when something should have been done and hence no further time should be wasted before conducting an in-depth study of the situation. The resultant recommendations should then be acted upon at once; otherwise the will of the people and the intent of the Constitution will continue to disappear in the giant federal bureaucratic maw.

As things stand now, our democratic form of government, in its most fundamental sense, is in danger. I only hope that what I have said here will underscore the importance of understanding what we are up against and encourage those in positions of responsibility to take some courageous and drastic action to meet it effectively.

V / Federal Workers, the Bureaucracy, and Individual Freedom

Almost half the new jobs being created these days are in government—federal, state, and local. The total in 1976 will exceed 14 million, and will cost the taxpayers an estimated $135 billion for salaries and fringe benefits.

As the hiring rate steadily increases, one question that arises is: How long can the nongovernment workers support Uncle Sam's work force?

The biggest question, however, involves the ever-growing power of unionized bureaucrats. The number of union-organized public employees has burgeoned in recent years, as has organizational "know-how."

Let me give you an idea of what I mean: In 1954 the total number of federal, state, and local government workers was 6,751,000. That figure jumped to 9,596,000 in 1964, and to 14,845,950 in 1974. And union organizers kept pace with the growing payrolls.

During this twenty-year period bureaucrats on all levels of government acquired great gobs of new power from the Congress. While it was illegal for federal employees to strike, state and local government workers were not so enjoined, and they obtained additional power through strikes. In 1954, there were only 15 strikes among these state and local workers, involving 7,000 people throughout the whole nation. By 1973, however, the number of strikes had grown to 386 and involved 196,000 public payrollers.

What's more, Congress seems to have given up on the argument that government—12 million state and local and 2 million federal—workers don't have the right to strike. As former Rep. J. R. Waldie (D–Calif.), an ex-member of the House Civil Service Committee, put it:

"It's nonsense to talk about the right to strike for government workers as if such a right could be denied them. Granted or not by law, it is a right that is going to be exercised."

The bureaucrats I want to deal with here are the ones in the federal government who will program the middle-management programmers in the social-management area mentioned in the last chapter. Actually, they are the aristocracy of the unionized government employees. They have long experience in the federal machinery and all the money needed to "put their show on the road."

In addition, they have the most sophisticated equipment to work with. Besides electric typewriters, offset printing machines, Xeroxes, and so forth, they have some 26,000 computers in the 300,000 buildings they occupy throughout the country. Their paperwork costs last year totaled $16 billion, and in this connection, the Pentagon alone, according to the best estimate available, shredded over ten billion dollars' worth of secret government documents.

To appreciate these figures, we have only to realize that President Franklin Roosevelt's Brain Trust was astounded back in 1942 to learn that the federal bureaucracy had grown to 1,600,000 employees. As a result FDR got the Congress to pass a bill aimed at minimizing the red-tape burden falling on taxpayers and business. The law was passed and signed, but today it just sits there as something of a monument to the government's disinclination to do anything about the "paper blizzard" of new forms coming out of Washington day after day.

The Office of Management and Budget estimates that organizations and individuals have to spend 130 million man-hours a year to cope with the mounting glut of federal forms. American business, of course, takes first prize for the number of government forms it has to fill out; its paperwork, as a consequence, has increased by 50 percent since 1967.

Paperwork, of course, helps out the paper industry and creates new jobs. But it doesn't add to the country's Gross National Product or industrial output. Instead, what too often results is nothing but wasted time and expense and unusable data to be stored in those 300,000 bureaucratic buildings.

But the paperwork blizzard is nothing compared to what could happen to this country if all public employees obtain and use the right to strike. Congress has before it right now a measure that would permit federal workers to strike. When you take into consideration public workers at the state and local levels, this would mean that some 14 million public employees would be permitted to leave their jobs any time they felt a grievance. We could, with the kind of labor-controlled Congress we have today, see a nationwide rash of strikes that would cripple transit facilities, hospitals, and schools, or produce, nationwide, a garbage glut such as New York experienced some time back when the sanitation workers in that city decided to strike.

With the increase in power held by the nation's bureaucrats, there is a corresponding increase in the power of a labor leader named Jerry Wurf.

Wurf is the fifty-five-year-old international president of the American Federation of State, County and Municipal Employees (AFL-CIO). He is reported to be one of the most powerful of the nation's labor leaders. His union of gov-

ernment employees is the fastest-growing one in the country
and this spells big trouble for the taxpayer and more tur-
moil in public services for the future. Wurf is extremely
conscious of his power. He has his home wired like a military command post so that he can be reached immediately
by phone by his own staff or by the officers of over 2,600 of
the union's locals in the fifty states, in Puerto Rico, and in
the Panama Canal Zone.

Most of the people who make up the membership of
Wurf's union are unknown to the public at large, but they
make decisions or nondecisions that reach into the lives of
215 million Americans.

These petty decision-makers grant, withhold, or revoke
broadcasting and TV licenses; levy penalties on cheating
taxpayers; tell employers whom they must hire and how
much they should pay them. In the opinion of many observers, these bureaucrats are becoming the new bosses of
the United States without the public being any the wiser.

People who are aware of the public-employee situation
actually wonder whether it has gotten beyond all control.
And they might well wonder when it comes to the latest
fringe benefit that the federal employee unions are now
said to be considering. Since it involves sex—repeat, sex—
in a very direct way, labor circles are regarding it as "the
offer they couldn't refuse." The benefit was discovered by
Joseph Young, a columnist for the *Washington Star,* who,
"in a spirit of helpfulness," called it to the attention of the
unions.

Mr. Young acknowledged that the idea—certainly one of
the most esoteric and erotic ever to be considered seriously
as a legitimate fringe benefit—did not originate with him.
He says he got it from reading the *Labor Management Relations Service Newsletter,* the official publication of the

National League of Cities of the United States Conference of Mayors and the National Association of Counties.

The newsletter, knowing that the members of these groups are the officials who have to deal with the public employees' unions, called attention to a report from the Fiji Islands, which dealt with a gold miners' union in Suva and its demand for a fringe benefit known as the "nooners."

It seems the miners' union wants, as part of its current contract, a 30-minute mid-day "sex break" for its members.

The union secretary was quoted as saying that the miners believe mid-day is the best time for men and women to engage in sexual relations, and union officials reportedly are arguing that if a man comes home at 5:00 P.M. exhausted and dragged out from a full day's work in the mines, he won't be able adequately to fulfill his sexual obligations to his wife. Accordingly, the union is asking for a half-hour sex break *in addition* to the normal lunch period.

The union secretary also indicated that "alternate arrangements" would have to be made for bachelors. "We don't want to overdo this," he was quoted as saying.

It would appear that the labor movement in America has come a long way since the days of Samuel Gompers and the battle over child labor laws. I doubt if even John L. Lewis or Philip Murray ever heard of a fringe benefit called the "sex break." In all events, it seems to be here and I'll bet it's here to stay.

Some observers are inclined to believe that something can be done in Congress to curb the excesses of unionized public employees. Maybe it can, but the trouble is that Congress shows every indication of waffling on the question. What's more, the Congress is playing the same game with the same people by whom it is controlled. Let's take a look at where the Congress stands on the question of bureaucratic expansion.

A close study will reveal that everything in Congress has increased except its performance on behalf of the overburdened public. The budget and staff on Capitol Hill have swelled phenomenally. Although the total membership of the House and Senate remained virtually unchanged, everything else has skyrocketed.

For example, in 1954 Congress employed 4,500 people and operated on a budget of $42 million. In 1974 Congress employed 16,000 people and had a budget of $328 million. And let me tell you it takes more than the kind of inflation we've just had to justify a staff increase of 256 percent and a budget increase of 681 percent. Just to accommodate the physical growth of the staff, Congress has overflowed into two more buildings and has contracted for another $34-million office building.

At this rate, by 1984 it will cost $1 billion to operate Congress.

What results from the tremendous increase in congressional personnel is a comparable increase in the number of amendments suggested for major pieces of legislation. Most of the amendments are written by staff members, rather than by the senators themselves; in fact, few members know precisely what is contained in or what might issue from these amendments. Consequently, there is an expanded volume of poor legislation.

The amendments also require a ridiculous number of roll-call votes, making it necessary for senators to spend so many hours on the floor that none of us can completely or properly do our committee work. In the first session of the 93rd Congress (1973), there were 594 yea-and-nay votes in the Senate and 307 in the House. In the second session of that Congress (1974), 544 yea-and-nay votes were taken in the Senate and 325 in the House.

This compares with 89 votes in the Senate and 71 in the House in 1953, my first year in the Senate. The tally for 1954, the second session of that Congress, was 181 in the Senate and 76 in the House.

This means there were 1,770 yea-and-nay votes during the 93rd Congress compared with only 417 yea-and-nay votes during the 83rd Congress in which I first served, an increase of 325 percent.

Legislative reorganization of the Congress in 1946 pared down the number of standing committees to 19 in the House and 15 in the Senate. Although the number of standing committees has changed very little since then (in 1974 there were 21 committees in the House and 19 in the Senate), a huge number of subcommittees have been created to take the place of the committees in 1946.

In the last Congress there were 147 subcommittees in the Senate and 133 in the House. There are 9 different committees handling environmental legislation; 5 studying the energy question; 3, plus a presidential commission, investigating the CIA. The Senate Judiciary Committee alone has 177 employees; the House Education and Labor Committee has 122. In his farewell address to the Senate, Sen. George Aiken (R–Ver.) chided his fellow members for this "unholy expansion of committees, subcommittees, and staff personnel which has mushroomed to an unconscionable extent during the last decade."

Public insight into this expansion is very limited. Although Congress oversees the budget of the entire federal bureaucracy—including the president's own staff—Congress alone, unchecked by any other authority, decides how much to spend on itself. In the same year that Congress passed a liberalized freedom-of-information act designed to give the public greater access to government bureaucracy records, it voted to close to the public the records of the foreign-travel expenses of House members and their staffs.

The *Washington Post* recently made an investigation into the staffing practices of Congress and had to use its IBM computer to sort out complicated congressional spending reports and so forth, in order to figure out what was going on.

It found widespread abuse of the committee system— members diverting staff hired for committee business to their own personal staffs; holding numerous "field hearings" to gain publicity in their own states; taking winter vacations, and avoiding payment of full travel expenses to places where they have speaking engagements; building presidential campaign organizations through the accumulation of congressional staff; holding hearings on subjects outside the jurisdiction of a committee.

For at least three-quarters of the time I have spent in the Senate, I have been harangued with the argument that the executive branch has too much power and more of it should be returned to the Congress. I have been told that members of Congress know more about what is going on in the country, and therefore are better able to cope with the problems which were and are confronting us; that the Congress—the Senate and House—know where to get the best staff members to cope with these problems; that we need a new cadre of men and women with solutions to our problems that have never before been tried.

It goes on and on. New staff people in a different segment of government—this time the Legislature—are held up by our liberal friends as the "last best hope on earth." Experience, we are told, is something belonging to the "old fogies" who got us in our present mess. They, according to our new liberal members of Congress, are the last kind of people we need.

One finds oneself actually wondering if experience in the affairs of men has anything to do with knowledge and wisdom. Then one comes to understand a basic truth: The problem is not ideas, or concepts—it is men and politics.

But the huge increases given Congress in men and money haven't satisfied all of the liberals. Men like Ralph Nader, for example, would like to see a bureaucracy on Capitol Hill that could rival the one working in the executive branch of government downtown (in Washington) and throughout the United States. That's the only answer they have when one tries to pin them down concerning their criticisms of the federal bureaucracy and how it operates in their particular field of endeavor.

This idea may hold some attraction for new, young legislators who see themselves serving as "straw bosses" or "ramrods" to huge congressional staffs comparable to the top-heavy bureaus and departments of the executive branch. But it strikes me as the surest way to wreck the Republic financially in a welter of bureaucratic nightmares the like of which the world has never seen before. For this entire process concentrates more power where there is already too much power.

Many times, both publicly and privately, I have complained that too much authority—important authority—is left in the hands of congressional staff members who have no right, and in many cases no ability, to exercise it. I'm not saying that every member of a staff—whether the staff is that of an individual Senator, a House member, or a committee—is inefficient. Far from it. Most staffers are extremely able. But this does not alter the fact that they have been given far too much power by members who are too busy or too lazy to exercise it themselves. This is not right. Nor is it, as I pointed out previously, in keeping with the governmental structure envisioned by the Founding Fathers, because these staff members often exercise the power of decision-making on matters affecting millions of Americans, although they were never elected to do so.

Should there be an explosion of staff help on Capitol Hill (that is, in the U.S. House and Senate), the power of that army of nameless, faceless bureaucrats would be multiplied many times.

From my own experience (and remember, I come from one of the smaller states as far as population is concerned), I can tell you that even now the members themselves are hard put to handle their legislative chores while riding herd on committee staffs and their problems. And what happens if the chores on Capitol Hill become too much for the members *and* the staff people they have assisting them? The next step will be to computers. That may sound like the perfect answer to some, but I see it as a gigantic step toward complete invasion of the privacy enjoyed by American citizens.

According to calculations made in 1967, the government alone kept 3.1 billion records on individual Americans. These were stored in at least 1,755 different kinds of federal agency files. But those who value their privacy had better get ready for what's ahead—a data-bank society. Right now, details of our health, our education, our employment, our taxes, our telephone calls, our insurance, our banking and financial transactions, our pension contributions, and many other personal matters are being stored in computer systems. And unless these computers are specifically programmed to erase unwanted information, these details from our past can be reassembled at any time to confront us.

Americans don't realize that revolutionary changes in data storage have taken place or are imminent. Some devices now exist which make it entirely practical to record thousands of millions of characters of information, and to have the whole of this available for instant retrieval. It is entirely possible for individual Americans to lose their anonymity without even knowing it. Indeed, a new political issue is emerging in the wake of the Watergate scandal because people are becoming ever more alarmed at the centralized use of personal information.

The enormous growth of the federal bureaucracy has obscured the right of the American citizen to even a minimum degree of privacy, not only from government agencies, but also from commercial groups that make it their business to know other people's business.

For some members of the Congress, the privacy of the individual has become a nearly full-time preoccupation. In fact my son, Barry Goldwater, Jr., has devoted a very great deal of his time to legislation that would control the assemblers of data on ordinary law-abiding people. The exact amount of such data collected by the federal government is shrouded in mystery. For example, a subcommittee of the Senate Judiciary Committee that has spent four years studying the problem is preparing a 4,500-page description of the process and puts the number of federal data banks at between 800 and 900. More than fifty different federal agencies are involved.

To cap the whole question of data collection on individuals, the General Services Administration is proposing a new nationwide computer system that would involve 100 million dollars' worth of new equipment which would replace sixty older computers now run by the GSA and the Department of Agriculture. While concerned members of

Congress contend that the system would allow the government to assemble dossiers on any individual or institution, the GSA says an elaborate system of "passwords" and code numbers would prevent one section of the new system from getting into other sections.

When all is said and done, however, the paramount question is how to control people who control data.

But if the data collectors are threatening the privacy of the individual, the enormous tax burden is threatening his solvency. The total amount of taxes paid to local, state, and federal governments has risen 781 percent since 1944. Today the government takes more than one-third of every dollar of income generated in the United States. This means that the average person spends three hours of his average working day paying this tax bill—more than he spends for food, clothing, and shelter.

With this huge and growing tax burden, the government is encroaching more and more into areas previously left to personal choice. We ride monopolized and government-regulated city transit, commuter railroads, taxicabs, airlines, buses, and trains. Our raw materials are delivered and our products are shipped by regulated trucks, trains, barges, and pipelines. Our homes are heated by government-regulated gas. We drink government-regulated water. We read by government-regulated light. Our food is inspected by a government agency. The drugs we take are tested, and in some cases prescribed, under government supervision. The government can limit the amount an individual can spend per child on education, how much he can contribute to political candidates, and how much he can spend—out of his own pocket—on his own political candidacy.

In the area of private business, the government has something to say about where a business can build, how it must design its buildings, whom it can hire and promote, how much it must pay employees, what standards its products must meet, how it can advertise its products, how much it can sell them for, and with whom the firm can merge.

These trends are hardly on the decline. Since 1970—six short years ago—three new major independent regulatory agencies were created which have across-the-board powers relating to every business. Two more regulatory agencies were proposed: one which could conceivably keep a firm from going out of business if closing down were considered "economically unjustifiable," and the other to dismantle corporations regarded as being too large or too powerful.

And now let us look at some examples of the infringements on personal freedom in the area of education.

American education is being quietly transformed—and the last vestiges of community control stripped away—by recent court decisions that communities may no longer support their schools through local property taxes. Starting with the California Supreme Court in 1971, many state courts have ruled that the financing of schools through local property taxes violates the principles of equal education and equal protection, because it results in the wealthy having more money to spend on education than the poor. As a result, states are being forced to institute the financing of schools. Through this system, the state government decides how much each community will be taxed for schools, collects the money, and then redistributes it in such a manner that no school system is better off than any other. The impact of this on individual communities can be devastating, as the following shows:

   New Trier, Illinois: This wealthy community has lost
      the right to tax itself *at a higher rate* in order to sup-

port its superior local school system. The state required New Trier to *cut* its local school taxes in order to equalize its educational output with the rest of the state. New Trier must now fire thirty-five faculty and staff members, and the school superintendent told *The New York Times* that this would "make the quality of our education decline drastically."

Grosse Pointe, Michigan: In accordance with a 1973 state education law requiring all school districts to produce an equal educational "yield," this school district must fire some of its faculty and trim its curriculum. Fifteen miles away in Garden City—a less-affluent, blue-collar neighborhood—the schools are hiring more teachers and expanding their vocational-training programs with the extra income from school-tax redistribution.

Wiscasset and Portland, Maine: The state of Maine cut school taxes in poor districts and raised them in wealthy districts. The taxes are now redistributed from the wealthy to the poorer school districts. In Wiscasset, the town must turn over one-half of the $2 million it collects annually in school taxes to the state government. In Portland, the superintendent told *The New York Times* that because they are a more affluent district they now receive less money for their schools and hence must lower the current quality of education, or "dismantle the school system."

The Connecticut Superior Court ruled in January 1975 that local property taxes violated the equal protection and equal education clauses of its constitution. In 1973 the state court of New Jersey ruled that supporting local schools through local property taxes gives unfair advantage to the wealthy.

Some states, however, still allow wealthy districts to tax

themselves at a higher rate in order to maintain their superior school systems.

In 1974, for the first time, local revenues were responsible for less than one-half the money spent on American public education.

During my first two terms in the Senate of the United States, stretching from 1953 to 1964, I served on the Subcommittee on Education of the Labor and Public Welfare Committee. I constantly resisted, with all the vigor I could muster, federal aid to elementary education. Naturally, I was stamped as a person with archaic views opposed to education. This, of course, was totally untrue, but the accusations militated against my arguments and the damage was done.

The danger I was trying to point out, particularly to the American mother and father whose children were in school, was that with federal money went federal control; but I could not make Americans understand what it was going to do to the educational system of this country. I was so soundly defeated in 1964 that the Congress took part of that defeat as a mandate to give President Lyndon Johnson everything he asked for, and he was asking for federal aid to elementary education. His request was granted, and as a result, control of what our children are taught was taken from our hands. And while in the years following 1964 we saw governmental expenditures on elementary education rise, we also saw the quality of education steadily deteriorate.

Anyone who tries to argue that elementary education or—let's put it another way—that the average product of the average grade school and high school system of this country is equal to what it was ten or twenty years ago just hasn't taken the trouble to study the facts. Students are being turned out with little or no attention being given to what they have, or have not, learned. To put it as bluntly as I can, the American people and their children are being victimized by federal control of tax money spent on elementary education, because our system of education is ailing to such an extent that it may be on the verge of collapse.

The federal power responsible for this tragic situation has been pushed down the throats of the American people by a Congress suffering from mandate problems and goaded on by a union of teachers dedicated to the concept of central control of education; and I doubt if that body has, or ever will have, the gumption to take another look at federal aid to education from the viewpoint of those of us who claim that a dollar spent at the local level, supervised by the local parent, teacher, and parent-teacher organization, produces a far, far better system and student than anything coming from, or controlled by, government people thousands of miles away.

Hopefully, at some time in the future, a president with the proper attitude toward education will come along. If he wins in a big way, maybe the Congress will recognize the huge vote of the electorate as a mandate to them to take another look at the disastrous position into which American education has worked itself with the constant aid of the federal government.

VI/The Regulators

On February 1, 1975, a prominent economist, Thomas G. Moore, of Stanford University, charged during an ABC-TV special on the regulation of transportation that the procedures and red tape in the Interstate Commerce Commission (ICC) are costing Americans $10 billion.

Two days earlier another regulatory agency, the Federal Communications Commission (FCC), had destroyed a Midwest communications business by refusing to renew five of its licenses to operate radio stations.

About the same time, the Food and Drug Administration (FDA) was putting the "kiss of death" on two products sold by one of the nation's largest pharmaceutical firms.

Regardless of whether the economist was correct and regardless of how well founded the agencies' claims against the businesses were, the thing that bothered me about these actions was the federal government's using every conceivable excuse for sticking its nose into the American competitive enterprise system.

Some people, including some of my colleagues in Congress, seem to think I'm joking when I point out that if a close watch is not kept on the "regulators," it is possible that the federal government will regulate the nation out of business. Well, let me tell you it is not a joke, and anyone who thinks otherwise can check the rate of business bankruptcies in recent years and the reasons given for these failures.

Let me give an example of what I mean. A recent survey by the Office of Management and Budget, on the number of reports required of businesses from just a few federal agencies, shows that in the summer of 1975, 2,178 different ones were demanded, which took American businessmen the equivalent of 35.6 million man-hours to fill out. In late July 1975, Secretary of Commerce Frederick B. Dent told me that by that time the number had increased to 3,000.

Let's assume the average hourly wage for all businesses in the United States is $3 (actually, it is much higher). In this case, the cost to business for handling the new paperwork projects would run somewhere in the neighborhood of $105.8 billion, with this sum coming out of company profits, which are ordinarily used to create new jobs.

Government regulators never seem to get around to recognizing the effect of their actions on the job market and the economic health of the nation. President Ford put the problem in its proper perspective when he estimated that the annual cost to American consumers of unnecessary and wasteful regulatory policies is $2,000 per family. This means the total cost to the public is an estimated $130 billion.

Mr. Ford says he wants small business released from the shackles of federal red tape and needless paperwork. Pursuant to that suggestion, Sen. William Proxmire has introduced legislation which would end the use of all government forms unless they are approved by the General Accounting Office.

However, the job of deregulation, which is being called for on all sides, will require more than a simple bill of

denial. It must be realized that such attempts will be
fought bitterly in the labyrinths of bureaucracy by a small
army of policy-making employees. The total number of
federal regulators at this writing is 63,444 and the number
is increasing every month. Included in this figure are the
following:

Agriculture Department—animal, plant health inspection; Packers and Stockyards Administration	14,054
Food and Drug Administration (FDA)	6,405
Labor Department—employment standards, occupational safety	4,715
Treasury Department—Bureau of Alcohol, Tobacco and Firearms	3,760
Federal Energy Administration	3,125
Interior Department	2,851
National Labor Relations Board (NLRB)	2,454
Equal Employment Opportunity Commission (EEOC)	2,189
Securities and Exchange Commission (SEC)	2,086
Transportation Department—highway, rail safety	2,079
Interstate Commerce Commission (ICC)	2,061
Federal Communications Commission (FCC)	1,971

Federal Trade Commission	1,569
Federal Power Commission	1,320
Other Agencies	3,602

The above list and the conclusions drawn in this chapter are confined to the so-called old regulatory agencies, ones that have been in existence thirty-five years and more. A whole new family of regulatory agencies, which came into existence in the 1970s, will be dealt with in a later chapter. These include the previously mentioned Environmental Protection Agency (EPA), the Occupational Safety and Health Administration (OSHA), and the Consumer Products Safety Commission (CPSC).

The businesses regulated include just about every line that human beings engage in to make a living. The big one does what has to be done—hires enough accountants and paperwork experts to tackle the job; the little guy puts up a fight, but eventually goes out of business. For failure to comply with federal directives, each risks fines, jail, or both.

We seem to have forgotten that the free competitive enterprise system was once regarded as unique in America. Here in this country is where it was allowed to flourish and bloom. Here is where it has had its best chance to succeed—that is, until Uncle Sam began to interfere in it. Now the free enterprise system, this display-stone of democracy, is being whittled down by government regulations which carry the force of law, even though Congress might not have had anything to do with their formulation. As a matter of fact, most of our government regulations, as I've already pointed out, are set up by nonelected men and women in the regulatory agencies who contribute to the rules and requirements—affecting every man, woman, and child in this country—that are put out every year in the name of the federal government.

Through the Federal Trade Commission, the government has something to say about what manufacturers can tell the public about their products. The FTC's original purpose was to investigate only anticompetitive business practices; but its powers were expanded in 1938 to include investigation of deceptive advertising and consumer fraud. "Advertising" means any method by which sellers induce customers to buy their product.

The FTC also appears to be going the way of the FDA—using "truth in advertising" to require manufacturers to prove the "effectiveness" of their products. The FTC also has power over all warranties, which must be labeled either "partial" or "full." To be so designated, a warranty must then meet a specific government standard. The FTC recently won the right to investigate warranties issued not only by corporations, but by *individuals* or any size *partnership,* and by those "affecting commerce" not just those "in commerce."

Some examples of FTC decisions on advertising claims:

—It is misleading the consumer to call a fake fur a "fake fur."

—Discounters cannot advertise with the slogan, Buy One, Get One Free.

—A company cannot say its product is "better than" another product; but it can claim its product is the "best."

—A dime store had to label its turquoise rings to make sure the consumer knew they were not real turquoise.

—A toy company was forced to disclose that its toy did not fire real projectiles that exploded.

—First Prize Bobby Pins had to change their name because the FTC said it led consumers to believe they were eligible to enter a contest.

Recently, the FTC proposed to the Federal Communications Commission that broadcasters be forced to provide air time for replies to commercials. This proposal, however, was rejected.

The FTC budget has grown phenomenally—from just $4 million in 1963 to $45.5 million in 1976. University of Chicago law professor Richard Posner criticized the rulings of the FTC for imposing huge costs on the consumer by "impeding the marketing of cheap substitute products, including foreign products of all kinds, fiber substitutes for animal furs, costume jewelry, and inexpensive scents; obstructing a fair market test for products of dubious efficacy; and harassing discount sellers."

The Civil Aeronautics Board (CAB) is another regulatory agency rife with abuses. The Justice Department and four other administrative agencies are working together on proposed legislation to curtail the regulatory powers of the CAB, which, according to Justice Antitrust Chief Thomas E. Kauper, is responsible for the higher-than-necessary airline costs and fares.

To illustrate: Air Europe International announced that it was planning to start a Tijuana to Luxembourg service at a 70 percent cost advantage over current airline fares. Further, Air Europe contended that this service was outside the jurisdiction of the CAB because it would fly over, not in, the United States. Then the CAB announced a "notice of proposed rulemaking," which would amend the law to require that any air carrier operating aircraft of foreign registry must receive a permit from the CAB to fly *over* the United States.

If Air Europe is forced to fly around the boundaries of the United States, the resultant cost would wipe out the airline's proposed lower fare.

Now let's take a closer look at the Federal Communications Commission. The FCC has used its authority to protect the three major TV networks from competition by the cable-TV industry.

The first watershed decision was in 1966, when the FCC issued an order which had the effect of preventing cable-TV systems from importing distant signals to the nation's one hundred largest television markets. Also, cable TV was not allowed to duplicate on the same day programs carried on local stations.

The FCC modified these rules a trifle in 1972. But the principal gainers, according to Prof. Stanley Besen, writing in the *Journal of Law and Economics,* were the TV networks and television stations in the top fifty markets—where 90 percent of all broadcasting profits are made.

This situation, which permits regulation by fiat, has gone on for many years without any serious interruptions from either the Congress or the courts. Businesses and business organizations, such as the U.S. Chamber of Commerce and the National Association of Manufacturers, have made complaints with regularity but without success. Over the years they doubtlessly have been defeated by more articulate spokesmen on the left. What's more, they appear to be afraid to fight for their cause the way the unions battle for theirs.

Meanwhile, all other kinds of abuses of power are exercised by the regulatory agencies. For example, only recently it was discovered that a contract officer who helped write a ten-million-dollar computer contract for the Federal Power Commission once worked for the firm that won the contract. This is only a minor irregularity in the system.

What is involved here is an enormous area of law being written by men and women, *appointed* to their jobs, who may or may not have had sufficient qualifications to recommend the kind of regulations that would best serve the

American public. Some of the regulations are far more important than many of the laws passed by the Congress. For example, the Interstate Commerce Commission regulates everything that moves in commercial channels across state lines. The first regulatory agency ever appointed, it was set up before the turn of the century to regulate railroads and establish proper rates for rail carriers. Now, of course, it also includes truckers, airlines, and the like.

In a recent interview, the chairman of the ICC acknowledged that in arriving at freight tariffs, lower costs to the shipper (and thereby to the consumer) can be considered, but are *not* a major point.

The whole system of the commission's rates has become so complicated that one expert tried using a sophisticated computer to simplify the work of figuring them out. He told the American Broadcasting Company that he had spent five years just putting into the computer all the ICC tariffs affecting his company; and the job was not yet finished.

Very recently a new factor was brought into the regulatory picture when it was discovered that the members of the U.S. Civil Service Commission had been making job recommendations for vacancies arising in the federal system. For example, on thirty-five occasions in the past six years, the three members of the Civil Service Commission had recommended job applicants to officials in federal agencies. This, in effect, set up the Civil Service Commission as a small dictatorship that named the men who recommended the regulations under which American businesses and American consumers were forced to operate.

What's more, the Civil Service Commission reportedly has made a prime mess of the government's Upward Mobility Program, which cost the taxpayers $46 million during fiscal 1975. The program is intended to provide training and new career opportunities for lower-level federal employees.

This appraisal comes from the comptroller general after a survey of nineteen agencies which employ 92 percent of the federal work force. Here's what the CG reported:

1. Neither the Civil Service Commission nor the nineteen agencies had the data necessary to assess the mobility program's achievement, despite its high cost.

2. Only limited upward mobility has been attained.

3. Ten of the agencies "had not initiated significant effort."

4. Some agencies might have violated the law in setting up their programs.

5. In nine agencies that had initiated significant effort, programs were poorly structured and inefficient. "Employes with unused skills were not identified and other employes were offered training they did not need."

6. "Target jobs were not identified or made available to enable employees to use training provided."

7. "Training and education appeared to be overemphasized and many participants dropped out."

8. "None of the agencies had developed or followed adequate planning procedures."

9. "CSC guidance had not emphasized the importance of agencies determining at the outset the extent of their upward mobility problem . . CSC guidance on counseling was lacking."

10. "CSC lacked or did not use valid criteria to assess program results."

It has been known for a long time that something is radically wrong with the nation's regulatory system and I believe that is why the most popular section of President Ford's 1975 address on inflation to a Joint Session of Congress was that which called for the creation of a national commission on regulatory reform. The congressional response to this recommendation was at least enthusiastic, and seven bills were immediately introduced to carry out the recommendations. Whether the reform commission will be able to do the job properly is a matter in which every member of Congress should take an interest, and which every concerned citizen should study carefully.

And as the spotlight begins to focus more and more on regulatory agencies, the Civil Service Commission comes in for more charges. For years the commission has been regarded as a little above the ordinary government bureaucracy, since it was initiated to protect the government from the evils of the spoils system, wherein the winning political party practically emptied the government payrolls and filled them with its own people. But that was many years ago and now the Civil Service Commission has actually become part of the bureaucracy over which it was once expected to act as a watchdog.

The CSC is always quick, when confronted with charges of dereliction, to point out that abuses of the merit system attract newspaper notice but little is said about underabuse by responsible officials. Commission officials claim that 25,000 bureaucrats are dismissed annually for ineptitude, inefficiency, misconduct, or unwillingness to relocate. However, a little probing shows that most of these dismissals are of employees in their first year of work, which is a period of probation. It is after probation that a bureaucrat is protected, not only against politically motivated dismissals, but—in actual practice—against other grounds as well.

At the very least, there will be confusion galore when the regulatory reform commission goes to work. The airlines, for instance, are controlled by the CAB under the Federal Aviation Act. They are told, to name just a few items, what new carriers can enter the market, how routes are to be distributed, and how much can be charged in rates. The upshot is that in areas of routes and rates the element of competition has disappeared. But in the area where it does exist, the airlines' concentration of effort is on the one un-regulated aspect of activity—customer service. As one CAB official put it: "That's why the average airline TV commercial looks like an ad for a combined bawdy house and dinner theater."

All the customer can do is sit back and serve as a member of a captured audience, unable to state a preference between seeing a movie and keeping his money. He might also rather "brown-bag it" from New York City to California, instead of having the usual round of beef au jus on a plastic plate. But he is being asked to pay up for selections of entertainment and food made on his behalf by someone in a hurry.

But these items are petty compared to the direction the CAB is likely to take in the near future. For this quasi-official agency is moving toward the raising of airline prices in the previously unregulated charter market. Not long ago, it approved discussions between scheduled and charter carriers in the hope that an agreement could be reached on a rate floor for charter flights.

What this would amount to—no matter what the bureaucrats would like to call it—is a deliberate case of prices being pushed up by government regulation.

But ask yourself what the "regulators" are expected to do in a diminishing market. The ICC is a case in point.

This regulatory body was created back in 1887, presumably to protect shippers from the monopolistic tendencies of the railroads. But as early as 1935 the United States had grown a network of highways, and truckers were cutting deeply into the markets of the railroads; thus the need for protecting shippers from a railroad monopoly no longer existed. Yet the ICC still holds authority to investigate changes in the railroads' rates. What this means is that entry into the shipping market by new trucking firms is restricted by the ICC and at the same time rates are being fixed by carriers that are given antitrust immunity to do so.

The foregoing examples of agency operations were taken from a report on "government regulation" published recently by Lewis A. Engman, former head of the Federal Trade Commission. Mr. Engman, incidentally, was not typical of the average government regulator or federal bureaucrat. He was a dedicated public servant who showed a genuine, deep-rooted concern for government regulation (he has made a study of the entire process), and what it does to the American consumer—the very group the regulators were set up to protect. He recognizes the fact that today's ICC's regulatory machinery was originally instituted to ensure that interstate carriers are efficient, clean, and everything else the American consumer has a right to expect from this regulated industry.

Certainly no interstate carrier need be excessively concerned about new competition, Lewis Engman wrote. The ICC has not approved entry of a new truck carrier into the market since 1938. And just last month the CAB rejected an application by Laker Airways, a privately owned British airlines, to fly regularly scheduled New York–London flights for $125 each way.

Engman concedes that his article deals in depth with

only two or three particular instances of government regulation. Then he adds:

"But when you take all of the industries subject to direct federal regulation—that's air, rail and truck transport, power generation, television, radio, the securities and others—it works out to a substantial fraction of the economy. In fact, it is estimated that these regulated industries account for 10% of everything made and sold in this country. What makes them even more important from the point of view of inflation is that they tend to be industries whose costs show up buried in the prices of hundred of other products.

"In transportation, for example, when you change the price of hauling freight, that change is going to show up, not just once, but again and again. By the time you get a piece of meat from the pasture to the plate, it carries with it numerous transportation charges."

The regulators, in the beginning, were named to protect the American consumer. They have not only failed miserably in this task, but have succeeded in seeing to it that much of today's regulatory machinery actually shelters the producers from the normal competitive consequences of lassitude and inefficiency.

In some respects, of course, the bureaucratic hold has changed, reducing the original threat of abuse. In others, the regulatory machinery has simply become perfected. And, of course, in still others the installation of machinery was a monstrosity from the start and still is.

In all events, the consumer—however he is being abused —is paying through the nose, and paying plenty, in the form of government-sanctioned price-fixing.

According to Engman, direct regulation of industry is only part of the story. He points out that there are, in addition, dozens and dozens of federal and state regulations, all of which subvert competition in the name of a greater objective. Of course it is very often difficult to see exactly what the objective is or on whose judgment its greatness rests. Engman listed regulations such as:

1. State laws which prohibit advertising the prices of eyeglasses or prescription drugs.

2. The Jones Act, which forbids foreign competition in the shipping business between United States ports.

3. The federal government's own "Buy America" procurement preferences, which can allow domestic producers to charge as much as 50 percent more than foreign sellers for the same items.

4. An agricultural price-support program which asks the consumer to buy with his tax dollars what he does not want, cannot use, and will never eat.

5. An agricultural export subsidy program which asks the consumer to pay the farmer to sell his product to some foreign buyer at a price lower than that at which the consumer himself can get it.

The effect of some of these regulations may be seen in some recent events in California, where in the summer of 1974 the milk producers' association of that state dumped 420,000 gallons of fresh skim milk into Los Angeles harbor. The dairy co-op said this drastic action was necessary because there was no market for the milk. The critics of the co-op wonder what price was being asked when no customers could be found.

Engman charges that more products could be sold if it were not for the elaborate government programs designed to maintain higher-than-competitive prices on the producer, processer, and retail levels.

Mr. Engman said that the most distressing development is the pervasive and widely accepted dishonesty that envelops the government's approach to regulation. The existing crazy quilt of anticonsumer subsidies embodied in the intricately woven fabric of federal and state statutes and regulations is pernicious.

In most cases we have adopted the least efficient forms of the subsidies which cost the consumer so much to maintain. Their existence is deliberately hidden from the public or else their actual cost is obscured. Even the government has lost track of how much they cost and their responsibilities concerning them.

Every once in a while proposals are put forth to provide direct cash subsidies in lieu of the patchwork of regulatory subsidies that now blanket our economy. Each time, however, opponents rise indignantly to object that hard-working individuals and hard-working businesses don't want handouts. Like it or not, that is exactly what we're giving them now, whether it's called a cash subsidy or a regulation that does the same job.

Maybe our businesses don't want handouts. If they don't, I've wasted one hell of a lot of time listening to arguments in the Senate about how necessary it is to bail the Penn Central and Lockheed out of their monetary troubles.

Actually, I do believe there is an argument that can be used to end protests against Engman's claim that our airlines, truckers, railroads, electronic media, and much more of the business life of the nation are on the dole. It is this: We get all steamed up about wasteful and fraud-ridden welfare projects, and we certainly should, for if something isn't done in that area the handouts will eat us up. But I would be something less than honest if I didn't point out that, by comparison, our complex system of hidden regulatory subsidies make the welfare frauds look pretty much like petty larcenies.

In his well-thought-out article Engman spoke of "free market purists" who are revelling in the growing disenchantment with heavy-handed regulations. They see the public all of a sudden waking up to their point of view: that the market is the fairest and most rational allocator of resources and its performance cannot be improved by regulation.

These arguments, taken to their extremes, are both naive and destined to be ignored. They're naive because they stress only the virtues of the long-range adjustment facility of the market system, while ignoring the short-term dislocation that market forces produce. They also discount the legitimate social objectives that enlightened people choose to pursue. As Mr. Engman put it, "Voters do not live on bread alone. And to the extent that they do live on bread, it is this year's bread, not next year's."

The "wrecking-by-regulation" of the Midwest communications company, referred to at the beginning of this chapter, was the most severe licensing action ever handed down by the FCC since the creation, in 1927, of the Federal Broadcasting Commission (it became the Federal Communications Commission in 1934). The decision was reached by an FCC vote of 5 to 1, and reversed a 1973 decision by administrative law judge Chester F. Naumowicz, Jr. In dissenting, Commissioner Robert E. Lee cited Naumowicz' recommendation that something less than a "death sentence" had been called for.

Charging that the stations had been involved in "serious misconduct" over a period of years, the FCC denied license renewals to five radio stations wholly owned by the same parent corporation, Star Stations, Inc., which, in turn, is owned almost entirely by businessman Don Burden of Omaha, Nebraska. Ironically, the FCC ruling was based primarily on the alleged favoritism shown by the five stations to the liberal political candidates Sen. Vance Hartke (D–Ind.) and then-Governor Mark Hatfield (R–Oreg.) during their reelection campaigns of 1964 and 1966, respectively.

For example, one of the charges alleged that "political advertising was carried for 44 days free of charge" for Senator Hartke. In the Oregon contest, the commission found that the parent organization, Star, sent $1,000 to Hatfield's campaign, in violation of the federal law prohibiting corporate contributions to federal candidates.

It should be understood that I am not taking sides in the legal controversy involving the Star radio stations. In fact, from what I can determine, the stations *were* engaged in trying to assure the reelection of Hartke and Hatfield. But that's not the point so far as I am concerned and so far as this book is concerned.

My objection here is to a quasi-official bureau of the government meddling in the business affairs of a community and issuing regulations which carry the force of law. In the Star case, the government's action is especially repugnant because the effect was to put a thriving communications business out in the cold.

In my opinion, it would be a good thing to do away with government licensing for television and radio stations. I believe there is a need for regulation in this field, but it should be confined only to frequencies. Why should the government *give* a license worth a million dollars to any individual or group when the free enterprise system could determine this issue without the kind of problems licensing brings with it. Just for my own information, I should like to know how many congressmen have been involved in this highly profitable licensing act. I know of one very prominent one from Texas, but I am sure there are others.

The actions of the Food and Drug Administration offer another dramatic example of how the federal government's regulators interfere with the free operation of the supply-and-demand concepts of the American enterprise system. Every time the FDA labels a food element or a drug "dangerous" to the public health, it plays havoc with some segment of the private enterprise system. Because of this, one of the favorite jokes in the Department of Health, Education, and Welfare is that Uncle Sam is the regulator who wants to prohibit the sale of cyclamates because they *might* prove harmful to public health and legalize marijuana because it *might not* be harmful to the public health.

I'm not suggesting that the government shouldn't have some way of checking on new and possibly dangerous products. But I am suggesting that there is a better method to handle the situation if we just go to work and look for it. Until now, the machinery for federal regulation in this area is simply the result of years of hodgepodge actions which lack any resemblance to sound national policy.

In fact, the President's Council of Economic Advisors estimates that federal regulation of just a few industries—airline, railroad, truckers, natural gas producers, banks, and savings and loan firms—may add as much as $13 billion a year to their operating expenses. They believe regulation by the government should be cut back drastically just as quickly as it can be done.

I suspect that many officials in the government who are currently worrying about the economy would be surprised to learn there are "government-mandated price increases"

adding to the nation's inflation woes. Indeed, a Washington University economist named Murray L. Weidenbaum
has recently published a book by that name.*

Weidenbaum believes federal regulation is a major factor
and a "neglected aspect of inflation." The author was
quoted in the March issue of the magazine *Nation's Business* in an article on the problems Detroit has encountered
in the automobile industry recently:

"The design and manufacture of the 1973 automobile,"
he [Weidenbaum] explained, "was subject to 44 government standards and regulations involving about 780 separate test points which must be met on each car."

Then there is the case of what is becoming known in the
business community as "the railway fusee problem." The
way *Nation's Business* tells it, this is what happened:

Until 1970, Army Ordnance bought railway fusees, or
signal flares, from U.S. firms. Bristol Flare Corporation,
for example, supplied them for years to the Picatinny
Arsenal in Dover, New Jersey. Then, according to Bristol
president Reba Goebig, a letter arrived, saying the firm
would have to be inspected by the army. It seems an am-
munition factory in West Virginia had exploded and new
safety measures were being taken.

Although Bristol offered the army flares at 49¢ each on
the next contract, the offer was turned down because the
company flunked the inspection. A similar offer by Standard
Railway Fusee Corporation of Boonton, New Jersey, was
rejected for the same reason.

After much investigating, it was discovered that the
army expected Bristol and Standard to meet standards
drawn up for munitions-makers. Charles W. Gardner, vice-

Government-Mandated Price Increases (Wash., D.C.: American
Enterprise Institute, 1975).

president of Standard, said the proposed new safety measures would have cost a fortune—and "the standards just don't apply."

Needless to say Bristol and Standard lost the contract, as did every other American manufacturer of flares. The order went to Canada, where a firm there met the U.S. standards and manufactured the flares for 59¢ apiece. The total price for 111,150 army fusees made in Canada was $65,578.50; the original Bristol offer was $54,463.50.

But the whole business of government-mandated prices which add to inflation is not the whole story as far as government regulation is concerned, and there is a very good chance that the Congress will very shortly order an overhaul of the entire regulatory system. I'm sure this radical-Democrat-controlled Congress' reason for reform will not be the same as one I would prescribe, but any action to improve the system would certainly be welcome. My own feeling is that the regulatory agencies have no business writing rules which have the effect of laws and that the free enterprise system suffers tremendously from this privilege. However, the leftwing liberals who run the House and the Senate and their committees are more interested in efficiency. While I, too, am in favor of efficiency, I am more concerned with restoring and maintaining the fundamental operations of our government under the system of checks and balances created by the Founding Fathers.

It is entirely possible that the crash of a TWA jetliner in the Blue Ridge Mountains, with a fatality list of ninety-two, will be used as the reason why a streamlining of the Federal Aviation Administration (FAA) and other regulatory agencies is necessary.

The investigation into the Blue Ridge Mountain crash is believed to be the most exhaustive ever conducted by

the National Transportation Safety Board. The board
called forty witnesses, and from their testimony and the
evidence provided by 115 exhibits, compiled a 7,000-page
account of the crash. During the sixteen days of hearings,
there were indications that the smashup could have been
prevented had any one of several actions been taken, either
immediately preceding, or years before, the accident occurred. The FAA, which is charged by Congress with protecting the flying public by creating and maintaining a safe
air-traffic system, has exhibited a remarkable bureaucratic
resistance to positive action over the last seven years. According to a *Washington Post* account, the agency failed
to solve what both the U.S. Air Force and Trans-World
Airlines (TWA) had warned were confusing cleared-for-
approach instructions that FAA-regulated air-traffic con-
trollers were giving to pilots.

The charges involving the air crash came at precisely the
right time for those in the Administration, the Congress,.
and among the public who would like to reshuffle the
whole system of government regulatory agencies. There
seems to be little doubt that the agencies are in trouble
and the signs are easy to read. For example:

—The Civil Aeronautics Board recently withdrew its
controversial minimum charter-fare guidelines, which they
claimed represented illegal rate-fixing, to protect the interests of scheduled air carriers under the agency's regulatory
system.

—The Federal Trade Commission, which always has in-
sisted on its own law enforcement activities, has become
involved in the affairs of other regulatory agencies such
as the CAB, the Interstate Commerce Commission, and
the Federal Communications Commission. FTC spokesmen

also have been doing a great deal of talking lately about
the regulatory process and its hidden costs to the consumer.

—The Interstate Commerce Commission, the oldest
among the regulatory agencies, recently sent shock waves
through the railroad managements by blocking a 7 percent
freight rate increase. Spokesmen for the ICC said a major
factor prompting the action—which took even the opponents of the bill by surprise—was a desire to present a
public image of a regulatory agency not going along with
whatever the industry proposed.

There is no question but that the ICC and all the other
regulatory agencies that have such a powerful influence on
the lives of American citizens are beginning to listen hard
to the demands for reform. Unlike previous demands that
the agencies be revamped, this time a combination of factors—all of them important—are sparking the drive.

For one thing, the current criticism is not coming from
just a disgruntled individual or group unhappy about a
particular ruling, but from members of Congress, the public, and from within the Ford Administration. The complaints are becoming a steady drumbeat that spells more
trouble for these quasi-official agencies than they have ever
before experienced, and it is reaching its crescendo in the
midst of national economic crises over inflation, unemployment, and deficit financing.

Although the reaction varies from one regulatory agency
to another, there is a general easing of formerly issued
regulations all along the line, and commissioners are listening to complaints that a few months ago they would have
shrugged off as inconsequential.

Also, there are many signs that Congress is getting ready
for a fundamental debate on how far to allow the nation's

regulatory agencies to go in the formulation of rules that carry the same power as the laws that are passed by Congress itself.

These indications of change don't apply just to the regulatory phase of government power over American citizens. Similar signs are cropping up in other power-dispensing government areas. We can thank the Watergate scandal for that. If it hadn't been for the "breaking and entering" that went wrong at the Democratic National Committee headquarters, the nation's lawmakers, citizens, and newsmen wouldn't have developed the intense interest they have today in the power that stems from the taxpayers and is exercised by bureaucrats.

So all of this brings us back to Lord Acton's observation that "power tends to corrupt and absolute power corrupts absolutely." I'd still like to find an exception to his maxim, but my despair of ever doing so grows deeper the longer I am in public service. Instead, I'm inclined to believe that a proper and well-thought-out delegation of authority holds the answer we're looking for.

VII / Labor's Clout
in Government

Not all the power in Washington is wielded by Congress, the regulators, the bureaucrats, and staff experts. The heaviest clout ever held by a lobby for special interests in the United States is that belonging to organized labor today. In fact, some veteran observers believe that the multi-million-dollar investment by the unions in the 1974 elections has made labor the most powerful nongovernmental force ever to operate in the nation's capital.

A recent book by Douglas Caddy, the original attorney for the "Watergate Seven," gives a pretty good picture of what I mean. The book, entitled *The $100 Million Pay-Off: How Big Labor Buys Its Democrats*,* flatly labels the labor union operation in recent elections as "illegal" in a way that forms an ample basis for prosecution.

Caddy pulls no punches when discussing his book. In an interview for the newspaper *Human Events* on August 10, 1974, he charged that labor bosses now claim they control 57 out of 100 members of the U.S. Senate and 230 of the 435 members of the House of Representatives. This gives the United States a "labor Congress" that, according to Mr. Caddy, does not satisfy President George Meany of the AFL-CIO. Meany wants a "veto-proof Congress," which means a Congress in which labor controls two-thirds of

*New Rochelle, N.Y.: Arlington House, 1974.

the members of both Houses. In addition, Mr. Meany is determined to elect a "labor president" in 1976.

Conservatives in the Senate can predict to within one to three votes the outcome on almost any legislation backed by labor or by special-interest groups such as Common Cause. And one has only to look up into the galleries and see the faces of those who have a special interest to know when the issue is of special importance.

Labor's political power is so great that for years it has prevented either the president or the Congress from nullifying a law that costs the taxpayers billions of dollars every year. This little-known statute, called the Davis-Bacon Act, was passed in 1931 and requires minimum wages of as much as $100 a day for the 4.5 million members of the construction industry union. When Davis-Bacon was first enacted, its purpose was to prevent irresponsible contractors for government construction from importing low-wage crews from distant points to displace local workers. It directs the secretary of labor to set minimum pay rates at the level of wages prevailing in the immediate area. Contractors are informed by Washington what they must pay their workers before they even bid on a government job.

The act is so unfair, as well as inflationary, that the President's Council of Economic Advisors has gone on record as opposing its retention. Chairman Arthur F. Burns of the Federal Reserve System is also against it, as are many others.

But nothing happens because of the strong alliance existing between the labor leaders and their congressional and bureaucratic allies.

The president has the authority to cancel the law by executive order in the event of an economic emergency in the nation. However, that is a very extreme step and has been used only twice in the two-hundred-year history of this country.

Labor now certainly holds more power over the Congress than any other special-interest group in my experience. Old-timers on Capitol Hill claim labor's hold even exceeds the tremendous influence wielded by the powerful farm bloc, back in the days of "Big Ed" O'Neill, president of the National Farm Bureau Federation, in the early years of World War II.

Labor's enormous power in Washington disturbs me, but not as much as the way that power was obtained: It was purchased with funds from the fat union treasuries controlled by the labor bosses, who many times do not reflect the desires of the union rank-and-file members who own the money.

During the Watergate scandal, powerful segments of the news media created the impression that the only campaign abuses occurring in 1972 had been those of business corporations and the Republicans. I submit that my party has no monopoly on campaign irregularities. As a matter of fact, when I think back over the days of bosses like Pendergast, Hague, and others, I wonder if the Democrats didn't actually "write the book" on campaign abuses during the past fifty or sixty years.

Late in its investigation, the Senate Watergate Committee announced it was going to look into the political activities of top union officials. The release of this statement came as a complete surprise to all the union critics in Washington and throughout the country. For example, Reed Larson, executive vice-president of the National Right to Work Committee, expressed the opinion that if the committee went about such an investigation seriously, "the whole shape of politics in America would suddenly change."

While the committee's decision, in and of itself, was somewhat startling, most startling of all was the fact that the committee investigators said they wouldn't limit themselves merely to questions dealing with cash contributions— the type of questions union officials always have ready answers for—but would also ask the union bosses to give them a detailed rundown on contributions of "goods" and "services" as well. These are the multimillion-dollar expenditures the union officials don't like to talk about, for they come out of funds—extracted from workers as a condition of employment—which are spent on politics but never reported as political contributions by the union bosses. These "in kind" donations to Democratic candidates include union-supplied manpower, automobiles, machinery, and all kinds of costly equipment needed to run an effective campaign in today's political system.

Students of this problem, as well as expert observers such as labor columnist Victor Riesel, estimate these expenditures at between $50 and $60 million a year—even in nonpresidential years. That figure is based on some 30,000 pages of documentation introduced in a federal court case in Los Angeles to support charges by members of the International Machinists Association that their compulsory dues had been spent by union officials to back candidates the members opposed.

The Los Angeles evidence indicates political corruption by union bosses far beyond the scope that most people suspected. And if it can be used as a measuring stick nationwide, tens of millions of dollars are involved.

But if reform elements were basing their hopes on the Watergate Investigating Committee, they, as the Brooklyn expression goes, "shoulda stood in bed." The Ervin Committee, so far as we can find out, talked to a few people, sent out some questionnaires, and then dropped the whole investigation of labor contributors. Thus the casual observer is left with the impression that this area of politics contained no irregularity worth investigating.

If the reason for the short-lived investigation by the Ervin Committee has ever been made public, I am one of those who missed it entirely. But I am more inclined to believe that the leaders of the AFL-CIO were too busy grinding other more important axes in the Congress and couldn't be disturbed. My reference here is to the deal the Senate Democrats forced on President Ford in late December of 1974 as the price for passing the Administration's trade bill.

This one was really odorous. Even the *Washington Post,* which ordinarily sides with labor, held its nose, and in its lead editorial of December 28, labeled the operation a "squalid deal."

"In order to get the necessary votes for the trade legislation in the Senate," the *Post* editorial said, "the President has agreed to sign the notorious Energy Transportation Security Bill—a bill that is a monument to the greed of the maritime lobby and the influence of its massive campaign contributions."

The editorial went on to explain that the trade legislation, providing the authority for American negotiators to begin the next round of international trade agreements that are urgently needed to keep the channels of commerce open, was a matter of truly extraordinary importance. The *Post*, indeed, went so far as to say that now, more than ever, world prosperity depends on trade, even though inflation and recession may complicate matters.

There can be no doubt about the importance of the trade bill; nor can there be any doubt that the senators, such as Russell Long (D–La.), were playing politics with it and were well aware of its vital importance. This is the same Russell Long who received $32,800 in campaign contributions from the unions in 1974.

Forcing the president to sign the transportation bill was little more than a sop to organized labor, a price for the passage of a vitally needed bill affecting American commerce throughout the world. As the *Post* explained it:

> Despite its resounding title, that bill has nothing to do with security. You might more accurately call it the Fatter Maritime Subsidies Bill or the Seamen and Shipyards Christmas Present. It would require part of our oil imports—20% immediately, 30% by 1977—to arrive in an American flagship. American tankers are vastly more expensive to fill and to operate than other nations', but this bill relieves them of any need to be competitive. It deliberately creates a captive market, forcing shippers to use them regardless of lower rates on ships under other flags. The American citizen will get hit three ways. First, as a taxpayer he will have to put up more money than ever for subsidies to uncompetitive shipyards to build the tankers. Then, again as a taxpayer, he will shell out more subsidies to keep the ships running. Finally, as a consumer he will have to pay more for oil products when the oil companies pass on these higher shipping costs.

Time and again officials of the Defense Department have testified that this bill does nothing for our national security. On the contrary, the department feels that if these cargo-preference rules become widespread, they may interfere with the availability of tankers in times of emergency and actually damage our national security.

Labor groups, especially the AFL-CIO, have opposed the trade legislation from the beginning. They know that imports cost jobs. Their fear, though legitimate, is exaggerated, so they went on to support this sorry stratagem.

How did big labor obtain such clout in the Congress of the United States? How is it that union bosses can almost dictate the kind of legislation they would like to see on the law books?

The answer is simple enough. I don't think it's unjust to say that they "bought" the influence needed to turn the wheels in the House and the Senate. Let's take the last election, for example:

In a news briefing held by the National Right to Work Committee on March 25, 1975, it was revealed that, in their campaigns for reelection in 1974, thirty-three members of the House Education and Labor Committee, which handles all labor legislation, were the recipients of $429,632 in campaign contributions from big labor unions in 1974. Is it any wonder that most of these members support legislation to establish compulsory unionism in the public sector—an objective sought by the union officials who approve the contributions? As for the nearly half million dollars the members received, perhaps the unions felt it would take a large amount of campaign money this time around, since the latest public opinion poll shows that 83 percent of the American citizenry is opposed to compulsory union membership for public employees.

In making the union figures public, the National Right to Work Committee chided the national news media for devoting more of their attention to other sources of contributions. Hugh C. Newton, the committee's director of public relations, put it this way:

"It is interesting to note that a number of major national news stories in February were devoted to the $134,000 contributed to 126 House candidates by the trucking lobby and the $16,500 in last-minute contributions to 14 key members of the House Subcommittee on Transportation. . . ."

One highlight of the National Right to Work Committee's news conference was the revelation that big labor unions contributed hundreds of thousands of dollars to fourteen members of the Labor and Education Committee, and of these fourteen, all but one are on record as being in favor of one of the bills legalizing compulsory unionism for public employees. They voted for forced union membership in 1970 for postal workers, and received 15 percent or more of their total campaign contributions from unions involved in such legislation.

The aforementioned dollar contributions by labor and those listed in the breakdown below weren't reported by some vague "reliable source," as is so much of the news from Washington. No, indeed. These figures are official. They come from the clerk of the House, which, according to the law, has jurisdiction over such matters. The figures show what can only be called a fantastically high rate of campaign contributions for House races, even in closely fought contests. And, of course, labor's preference for Democratic candidates over Republicans has never been shown more clearly.

Here's the way the nearly half million dollars was divided among members of the House committee that handles labor legislation:

Michael Blouin (D–Iowa)	$36,900
Paul Simon (D–Ill.)	34,400
John Dent (D–Pa.)	29,275
Robert Cornell (D–Wis.)	29,175
Frank Thompson (D–N.J.)	26,300
Ron Mottl (D–Ohio)	23,830
Lloyd Meeds (D–Wash.)	22,550
Peter Peyser (R–N.Y.)	21,555
William Clay (D–Mo.)	18,850
John Brademas (D–Ind.)	18,700
Ted Risenhoover (D–Okla.)	18,600
William Lehman (D–Fla.)	18,550
Leo Zeferetti (D–N.Y.)	15,062
James O'Hara (D–Mich.)	14,300
Phillip Burton (D–Cal.)	13,050
Dominick Daniels (D–N.J.)	12,550
George Miller (D–Calif.)	12,000
Tim Hall (D–Ill.)	11,150
William Ford (D–Mich.)	10,650
Mario Biaggi (D–N.Y.)	7,400
Joseph Gaydos (D–Pa.)	6,450
Ike Andrews (D–N.C.)	6,250
Edward Beard (D–R.I.)	5,350
Patsy Mink (D–Hawaii)	3,560
Ronald Sarasin (R–Conn.)	2,350
Shirley Chisholm (D–N.Y.)	2,125
Al Quie (R–Minn.)	2,000
Alphonzo Bell (R–Calif.)	1,900
Marvin Esch (R–Mich.)	1,900
Augustus Hawkins (D–Calif.)	1,400
John Ashbrook (R–Ohio)	500
Bill Goodling (R–Pa.)	500
Carl Perkins (D–Ky.)	500

John Buchanan (R–Ala.)	–o–
John Erlenborn (R–Ill.)	–o–
Edwin Eshleman (R–Pa.)	–o–
James Jeffords (R–Vt.)	–o–
Larry Pressler (R–S.D.)	–o–
Virginia Smith (R–Nebr.)	–o–
TOTAL:	$429,632

It should be emphasized again that the money paid to the members of the House Education and Labor Committee was in "reported" contributions alone. This is extremely important where labor unions are concerned, since, as mentioned earlier, much of their help to candidates is of a nature that does not have to be reported. Reed Larson said the cost of these in-kind contributions, which union organizers routinely provide to favored candidates in cash-equivalent manpower and services, is believed to be in the range of ten times the actual cash contributions. Cash is only the tip of the iceberg.

While these contributions presumably were "legal," we have to ask ourselves the question asked by the National Right to Work Committee in a large quarter-page advertisement in the *Washington Star* of April 8, 1975: Can a committee of Congress judge legislation fairly if that legislation involves special-interest groups which have provided major financial help to the congressmen's campaigns?

Perhaps. But on the municipal level not long ago, it was disclosed that unions embracing a third of a million city employees provided major help to elect the man who had a decisive voice in determining their benefits. In commenting upon this, *The New York Times* said editorially, "Whether or not the law condones it, here is a real conflict of interest."

Do we have a fundamental legislative conflict of interest here, where congressmen are concerned?

As a senator who has watched the labor scene closely for many years, I hasten to say there is no question in my mind that there is a *very grave* conflict of interest. The Education and Labor Committee in the House, aside from handling all the labor legislation which is introduced on that side of Congress, is currently in the storm's eye of a growing controversy over legislation which would put the federal government in the business of organizing public-sector unions, regulating the labor-relations policy of the states and their political subdivisions, and promoting compulsory unionism at all levels of government.

There is nothing especially new about big labor contributions to influential congressmen. For nearly forty years —ever since the enactment of the Wagner Labor Act under FDR—labor unions have enjoyed a special type of privilege and immunity at the hands of the legislators. And I am one of the first to say that when the Wagner Act was passed way back in the thirties it was long overdue, for American corporations had gone overboard in their unfair treatment of the American workingman. But now the pendulum has swung far in the other direction—much too far for the good of the free enterprise system and for the good of the country.

But if the labor unions showed favoritism to the members of the House committee which handles labor legislation, they did almost as well toward the members of the House committee that handles taxes, Social Security, and other matters of interest to big labor.

Official reports filed with the clerk of the House showed that the unions contributed a total of $233,779.21 to the campaigns of liberals who either were, or who wound up on, the House Ways and Means Committee. Yet they couldn't find a single Republican worthy of their financial support.

I haven't heard even one complaint or question about this strange situation, loaded as it is with conflict of interest, from the groups who are running around claiming they plan to get the power out of politics. But we certainly have enough organizations who have dedicated their efforts toward preventing giant corporations from working their will on the Congress.

The do-gooders who believe labor unions can do no wrong and corporations can do no good make me downright sick to my stomach with their righteous, double-standard politics.

Let me show you how union contributions to House races involving members of the Committee on Ways and Means ran in 1974:

1974 Union Contributions to House Ways and Means Committee

Democrats

*Richard VanderVeen (D–Mich.)	$50,852
*Abner Mikva (D–Ill.)	33,800
*Martha Keys (D–Kan.)	24,063
*Andrew Jacobs (D–Ind.)	18,650
Joseph Karth (D–Minn.)	17,150
*Henry Helstoski (D–N.J.)	13,350
*Fortney Stark (D–Calif.)	12,290
James Burke (D–Mass.)	10,950
*William Cotter (D–Conn.)	7,500
Dan Rostenkowski (D–Ill.)	6,000
Wilbur Mills (D–Ark.)	5,900
*Otis Pike (D–N.Y.)	5,900

*Joseph Fisher (D–Va.)	5,423
William Green (D–Pa.)	5,180
*James Jones (D–Okla.)	4,450
*Charles Rangel (D–N.Y.)	3,450
Al Ullman (D–Oreg.)	3,210
James Corman (D–Calif.)	2,860
Joe Waggonner (D–La.)	1,500
Phil Landrum (D–Ga.)	1,000
Richard Fulton (D–Tenn.)	300
Omar Burleson (D–Tex.)	–0–
Charles Vanik (D–Ohio)	–0–
*J. J. Pickle (D–Tex.)	–0–
TOTAL:	$233,779

Republicans

*James Martin (R–N.C.)	–0–
*Guy Vander Jagt (R–Mich.)	–0–
*William Steiger (R–Wis.)	–0–
*Bill Frenzel (R–Minn.)	–0–
*L. S. Bafalis (R–Fla.)	–0–
*Phil Crane (R–Ill.)	–0–
Bill Archer (R–Tex.)	–0–
Donald Clancy (R–Ohio)	–0–
John Duncan (R–Tenn.)	–0–
Herm Schneebeli (R–Pa.)	–0–
TOTAL:	–0–

*New members.

In the legislative branch, the power gained by labor in the 1974 elections is comparable to its gain in the 1936 election—the year FDR won the presidency by all but two states, Maine and Vermont—though its impact then was perhaps greater in the state legislatures. In Pennsylvania, where Democratic Governor George H. Earle was leading an administration called "the Little New Deal," enormous Democratic labor majorities were elected to both the House and Senate.

When it came time for the unions to draft a legislative program, the lobbyists for the United Mine Workers, the United Steel Workers, and the other powerful segments of organized labor followed their usual course. They demanded everything they could think of in the way of hours, wages, working conditions, and the like, expecting to get only a portion of the total package.

But this time, things turned out differently. About three-quarters of the way through the legislative session, the union leaders were amazed to learn that the lawmakers had changed so much that they (the unions) were in danger of getting *everything* for which they had originally asked. The labor lobbyists discovered that no one with any strength in the Pennsylvania legislature was opposing them, much less giving them a fight, and the bills labor demanded when the state lawmakers first convened were zipping toward enactment. The so-called Little New Deal was, in fact, coming into being. The arguments union organizers had traditionally used to recruit new members were being wiped out because the promised improvements in working conditions that had been their strongest selling points were rapidly becoming state law.

As one worker at the time put it: "Why join the union and pay dues to get a forty-hour week, a minimum wage, safety standards, and all the rest, when the state will provide them legally, for nothing?"

Why indeed?

The unions had asked for everything, and for once, they had a legislature that would give it to them.

That wouldn't do. So the Pennsylvania legislature saw

an amazing phenomenon at the end of the state assembly session in 1937. They actually witnessed state lobbyists for the large unions lobbying *against* major portions of their own legislative programs. It was a tricky operation but it was done and done successfully.

I recount this incident to give the reader an idea of what can happen when an arrogant majority gets control of both houses of a legislative body.

Our forefathers foresaw this danger when they drafted the U.S. Constitution. And they deliberately incorporated provisions to protect the minority under these kinds of circumstances. It may surprise some readers to learn that the Senate filibuster is an important segment of the legal wall erected against an overbearing majority in the legislative branch of government.

There really is such a thing as *too much* power in certain instances. Nonetheless, I am more interested in unused power where the federal government and labor unions are concerned. I say this in the wholehearted belief that labor unions serve an important purpose when kept within legal and reasonable bounds. Some of my friends will no doubt be surprised to read that I am in favor of labor unions, that I believe they perform an important function, and that I support their right to strike. It is my considered opinion that the strike is an expression of freedom on the part of the worker that must be protected. At the same time, I am opposed to compulsory arbitration because I believe that is a denial of freedom. And I am opposed to the growing demand for legislation for compulsory unionism at all levels of government.

What we need, and what I have urged on the Congress for at least fifteen years, is a national labor policy which would treat all segments of our society—especially big business, big government, and big labor—with an even-handedness not previously exercised.

Contrary to what many of my critics say, I have no desire to see America's labor unions abolished. Nor do I believe it would serve any useful purpose to take from the unions the gains they have made over the years against formidable odds. No, what I'm talking about here is a kind of balance among labor, business, and government that could benefit every single American.

But, believe me, this balance can't be achieved if liberals continue to give labor unions the advantage over all other economic groups. Granted, back in the thirties the labor unions needed help. Well, they got it—and they've been getting it ever since. They have now amassed enormous power in the federal government but they want still more. They want privileges, sanctions, and immunities that are enjoyed by no other segment of the economy.

Just to give the reader an example—the unions completely ignore the Federal Corrupt Practices Act which has been on the books since 1947 and under which corporations are prosecuted for making political contributions. In addition, the unions are not liable to the nation's antitrust and monopoly laws, although they apply to all business corporations.

Of course, the perfect time to have started bringing prosecutions against labor unions that had violated the Corrupt Practices Act was after Richard Nixon was elected president and Republicans took over the Justice Department and, with it, the machinery to bring legal action.

But nothing happened. The unions went their merry way, violating the law and electing to public office the people they wanted.

Then, little by little, it came out. President Nixon and

his political "Whiz Kids" had decided that if they played their cards right, they could woo organized labor into the Republican ranks.

This seemed to me so farfetched, I didn't pay much attention to it until the National Newspaper Guild endorsed Sen. George McGovern for president prior to the Republicans' convention to select their nominee. In short, the national leadership of the Guild had endorsed McGovern before it knew for sure who McGovern's Republican opponent would be in November!

The Guild's action was so outrageous—remember, the Guild represents most of the nation's political writers—I decided to call its members to task on the Senate floor.

As so often happens in Washington, word of my intentions got around before I was able to make the comments. And needless to say, I was flabbergasted when a staff man from the Committee to Re-elect the President called my press secretary and asked him if I would reconsider my remarks—because the Nixon people thought they could win the support of organized labor in the 1972 election if they handled matters right.

My answer (expletives deleted) can be found in the *Congressional Record* of July 19, 1972, under the heading "Newspaper Guild Shows Its Colors." It said in part:

Mr. President, during the past year we have heard an actual flood of words about freedom of the press and the public's right to know. The argument was used over and over again to defend the stealing of the Pentagon Papers and their subsequent publication by newspapers which knew they were printing classified government information.

Now, Mr. President, a question arises involving the press which I believe the public has a right to know lots more about.

I am speaking, Mr. President, of the apparent endorsement

of Democratic presidential nominee George McGovern by the American Newspaper Guild. This is one of the most interesting and least written-about stories that has come out of the Democratic party's convention and its aftermath. The question arises as to just what the Guild has done in this respect. All that I know about it was the story which appeared in the *Washington Evening Star* and *Daily News* of Friday, July 14th. It carried a Miami Beach dateline and was written by an anonymous "*Star* staff writer."

This story reported that Charles A. Perlik, Jr., president of the Newspaper Guild, walked into the McGovern press room the day before in the Doral Hotel and announced "the endorsement of our union for George McGovern as president of the United States and I appeal to you to support that candidacy as well."

According to the *Star* story, the room immediately exploded with political reporters disclaiming the action and demanding to know upon whose authority Perlik was acting. He said he was acting on a recent unanimous vote of the Newspaper Guild's fourteen-member executive board. He also told the reporters that it was time for journalists to stop being "political eunuchs," according to the story.

Now, Mr. President, I certainly have no wish to make a lot of enemies among the 33,000 reporters, photographers, and others who make up the Guild. However, if the Newspaper Guild is going to take a political position for the first time in its history, it's time that the American people who are dependent upon Guild members for their news are told all about it.

It is not enough, Mr. President, to say that this was a group "Freudian slip," in order to explain it away as merely the misguided action of an executive board.

In all fairness, Mr. President, the *Star* story said that within a few hours a petition was circulating at the convention headquarters expressing the "strongest possible disapproval" of the union action and promising further action to counter it. The petition noted that a reporter's political preference was a private and personal matter and that the press "is suspect enough" without the "outrageous arbitrary action" of its union officials.

Mr. President, it certainly is no secret that I am one who has raised not only suspicions but deliberate charges against some sections of the communications media for what I believe to be a built-in bias in favor of liberals such as Senator George McGovern, even as some members of the press are becoming self-conscious and critical of the image their associates are creating. The latest attack on Washington correspondents comes from none other than Robert Novak of the columning team of Evans and Novak and for years a reporter for the *Wall Street Journal.*

Novak let his hair down in a copyrighted paper he prepared for a symposium at Kenyon College which is later to be incorporated into a book called *Mass Media and Modern Democrats.*

Of the Washington correspondents Novak said this: "More and more, the members of the Washington press share a lot of the world views taken by the dominant liberals who control the Democratic Party." Novak said he sees "increasingly, a rigid conformity . . . among the Washington press corps" and "a startling consensus on the basic perceptions."

Interestingly enough, the *Washington Post* on Sunday carried nearly a page and a half in its editorial section on the press and its critics without ever mentioning the resolution reportedly adopted by the American Newspaper Guild.

Mr. President, the action of the Newspaper Guild, whether it runs into a protest petition or not, does not surprise me one bit. Many times I have referred to the liberal leaning of some sections of the American press corps and offered the opinion that it had its roots in actions taken long ago in the 1930s when the Newspaper Guild was first organized.

Despite my knowledge of the Newspaper Guild's background, I was amazed at its audacity in this instance. Representing working reporters as it does, I expected the Guild—in order to spare its dues-paying members any embarrassment—to emulate Caesar's wife, and not only be above political partisanship but avoid giving even the appearance of being otherwise.

I certainly agree with those who claim that the Guild's action should not reflect on all members of the Washington press corps. But at the same time I have to ask, What other conclusion can be drawn by neutral observers? Writers who put up with the Perlik kind of management have to sacrifice all claim to being objective reporters. It seems to me they have only three choices: to boot Perlik out of his job; to resign from the Guild, stating their reason for doing so; or to look the other way and pretend Perlik is not there and the whole sorry mess never occurred. Apparently most Washington political writers belonging to the Guild elected to take the last choice. I have seen no reports of large-scale resignations from the organization, and this indicates to me that the Guild members plan to go along with Perlik until some other kind of controversy shakes them up.

Since I am not a member of the Newspaper Guild, suggestions for that organization have little or no influence coming from me. But I am a member of the American body politic and, I hope, of the section that represents what is best in that group. To repeat, I believe—and I suspect many Guild members share my belief—that an organization representing newspaper people in any capacity should stay out of partisan politics. I also feel the Newspaper Guild modifies its punch by at least 50 percent by taking part in things political, and this is an effective way for Guild members to dig their own graves, professionally speaking.

While the foregoing is extremely important, it does not get at one of the major points of this chapter—the silly, almost comical, belief among the Nixon hierarchy that the Republican party could win the support of the nation's labor bosses in future elections. It is my considered opinion that such a process will take years, if it can be done at all. The rank and file of organized labor has had forty years of conditioning—call it brainwashing, if you like—in Democrat party principles. In some respects, although to a lesser degree, the labor rank and file resembles the voters of years ago in the South. Down there the GOP offered all the things they wanted, but voting Democrat was a habit so deeply engrained that it actually seemed to them a species of treason to vote another ticket.

What this all adds up to is the fact, mentioned earlier, that when the Republicans finally obtained control of the executive branch and the Department of Justice, no actions were brought to prosecute labor unions for the way they ignored the Corrupt Practices Act governing the questions of political contributions. For years, the unions have regarded themselves as special organizations, ones immune from the laws stipulating that corporations and labor organizations may not contribute financially to a political candidate. Since no one has ever been prosecuted under this law for a union contribution, the labor bosses have every reason to believe they are forever immune. When the Republicans had the opportunity to prove otherwise, they flubbed it.

And, of course, the unions continue to use the sometimes-more-valuable-than-cash device of in-kind contributions to whichever candidates they think will vote for labor's objectives. The Republicans, on the other hand, must actually beg their partisans for manpower, equipment, and assistance (such as doorbell ringers, large mailings, telephone blitzes, transportation to the polls, and baby-sitting services) for some of the most difficult tasks to be filled during a campaign and when election day rolls around. The Democrats get all these services free of charge from unions who pay the salaries of the people they send to help their candidates; therefore the helper has a lively interest in maintaining the candidates' operational expertise. And while the Republicans too often have to depend upon volunteer help, the helper from the union knows that in many instances his job is on the line, so he'd better get out there and do whatever job the union boss tells him to perform.

It is worthy of note that all the reforms by Congress to make the election laws fair and equitable fail to notice the disparity between in-kind political activities and those that have to be paid for. Perhaps this can be explained by the fact that the bill was put together by a liberal Congress. It does not surprise me; that is the way things are happening in the political capital of the world these days.

Because of its influence on lawmakers, the great power amassed by organized labor over the past years has contributed mightily to the recent runaway inflation and unemployment. It enabled unions to get wage increases for workers far in excess of their increased productivity. In other words, because of the immunity enjoyed by the unions, its members have stopped working harder to obtain benefits.

Federal Trade Commissioner Mayo Thompson believes if the average American was willing to work productively enough to raise our real output by 5, 8, or 10 percent a year, we could all have a corresponding increase in our individual incomes without inflation or higher rates of unemployment.

Thompson says the choice is: Settle for a 3 percent increase in wages and other forms of income, or buckle down and work harder.

But he sees trouble in labor unions that claim to speak for government workers. "Either we break the power of unions to demand and get wage increases in excess of our productivity growth-rate," he says, "or we're going to have inflation and unemployment into all the forseeable future."

Thompson argues, and I agree with him, that we are strangling the incentive to work in this country with a maze of labor and welfare laws that "take away too much of the carrot, and virtually all of the stick." All we have to do is look at Britain, he says, adding: "There you have a prime example of what is happening here."

Thompson says Britain is now, for all practical purposes, a nation ruled by labor unions. Economic power has been joined with political power. The workers, finding it more profitable in the short run to strike than to work, have succeeded in giving that country an inflation rate of just under 20 percent in 1974. Its more powerful unions demand—and get—yearly wage increases of even larger magnitude. And these, of course, are the same labor unions that have demanded—and gotten—a welfare system so oppressive that the British government now has to take more than 50 percent of the nation's gross national product in order to pay for it all.

There is no doubt that, in Britain's case, an empire that survived the assaults of all the great armies from Napoleon to Hitler has been brought down by an internal cancer, a rot created by a set of laws that encourages citizens to pool their capital. But why allow that pooling process to go on to the point where the last vestige of competition is stamped out?

I agree fully with Commissioner Thompson when he points out that the time when America's trade unions resided in run-down headquarters to wage the battle for union benefits belongs to the 1930s. Now most of them operate out of beautiful marble edifices, such as the one the money-heavy Teamsters Union maintains within walking distance of the U.S. Capitol. There is absolutely no reason why labor organizations that can build such large, mausoleum-type headquarters buildings in Washington should be given special treatment by the government. Instead, big labor is far better able to comply with the laws governing American corporations than many of the corporations themselves.

And why the unions should be exempted from meeting the provisions of the nation's antitrust laws I have never been able to understand. There may once have been a time when this made some sense from an economic standpoint. But that time was passed long ago when unions became big business.

VIII / The Social Security Mess

One built-in facet of the welfare state—Social Security —has given the gnomes, the money manipulators of Washington, an almost life-and-death power over millions of Americans. The problem affects citizens living on retiree programs or some other form of fixed income as well as the wage earner who has to meet his tax bill from Uncle Sam every year.

This is, without question, the most unfair and most devastating power wielded by anyone in America today, and that means anyone in or out of government. And it calls to account promises made in good faith by the government many years ago by men who never considered the possibility that the promises might not be honored.

The fact is the Social Security system, for all of the praise it received in FDR's day and for all the praise liberals have heaped on it ever since, is failing. Unless something drastic and unexpected happens, the United States government may be forced to go back on its word to millions of Americans who supported the program with dollars earned by the sweat of their brow for a period of nearly forty years.

The problem is money—it isn't there in sufficient quantities. Consequently, the gnomes are busily examining the monetary system of America to see if there is a way to finance the old-age retirement of Americans other than the one written into the original Social Security laws.

In the beginning, it should be recalled, FDR wanted a self-sustaining program. And that's what it has been until recent years. Taxes levied on the wage earner and the wage payer were combined to build a separate Social Security fund for the payments of benefits to Americans sixty-five years and over. And I believe this system could have worked if politicians had kept their hands off it.

But, no. It was too attractive a political target, and the demagogue types in Congress soon discovered that pushing legislation to increase and expand Social Security benefits was an easy way to "prove" their concern for the aged, even if tax money—yours and mine—was used to accomplish their purpose.

The outcome could have been, and was, forecast by congressional members worried about where deficit-financing was leading the country. But, as usual, those of us who cautioned about the future effects of this fiscal recklessness were ignored or ridiculed. We were even accused by proponents of the so-called new economics, which had their debut under President John F. Kennedy, of urging a highly dangerous policy. They argued—believe it or not—that balanced federal budgets and other fixtures of responsible government economics might throw the nation into an economic tailspin and wreck our society. In short, the proponents of the new economics felt that the United States had outlived the age-old "work ethic" of its past and should hurry right on to the failure-ridden, sophisticated mechanisms of Keynes running out of control.

It is because of this deficit-financing philosophy that the Social Security program is now in such deep trouble, and unless firm, positive steps are soon taken, it will not have adequate funds in 1976 to fulfill its end of the agreement it has with all of us who work for money. Already a government advisory panel has reported that the system will need an unprecedented government subsidy next year of $7 billion from general tax revenues.

In view of the fact that the Social Security law is really a contract between the federal government and its citizens, how can the advisory council ignore the contract's terms and recommend that Congress allow the system to dip into the general treasury? Characteristically, the council hasn't explained how they justify this breach of good faith.

On February 17, 1975, the magazine *U.S. News and World Report* reported that the system is "way out of whack" and that pressure is building up for a major overhaul "before the system drowns in red ink."

"Unless something is done soon," the magazine went on, "a small deficit in 1976 could balloon into a massive gap between benefits and taxes in just a few years."

In November 1975, the magazine *Nation's Business* built a story around Ida M. Fuller, a retired bookkeeper in Ludlow, Vermont, who had received the first monthly Social Security check ever issued. The year was 1940; the amount of the check was $22.54.

From that droplet, the flow of payments increased to a trickle, then to a stream, then to a river, and now it's a mighty torrent. In 1940 a total of $62 million went to 222,000 beneficiaries. By 1960 the system paid benefits to 14 million beneficiaries; in proportion to the number of workers—72.5 million—that worked out to a little over 5 to 1.

When the *Nation's Business* article was written some 95 million workers were providing benefits for 30 million retirees—a ratio of about 3 to 1. That ratio could easily be

2 to 1 by the turn of the century or certainly not long there-
after. The estimated number of beneficiaries by 1995 is
more than 40 million; ten years after that, it rises to 45
million; and by the year 2020, approximately 80 million.

In the immediate future the increase in the work force
will be affected by such unknown factors as the general
economic condition. But the cost-of-living increases that
beneficiaries will get next year, on the basis of the Consumer Price Index at the end of the first quarter, will be reflected in a higher wage base beginning January 1, 1976.
According to estimates in Washington, this base should be
around $15,300—which translates into a tax of nearly $900
each from the employer and the employee.

Most people on Capitol Hill admit that the whole Social
Security program is an economic horror which was not fore-
seen when Congress established the automatic escalator.
And as I travel around the country I hear more and more
grumbling on the part of young people, who object to the
amount deducted from their earnings for a program they
had no part in formulating.

Perhaps I may be forgiven if I am among the people
who will take a special interest in the way candidates for
public office, especially those seeking the presidency, handle
this Social Security issue in future years. I know from bitter
experience that it was a touchy issue in 1964. In fact it was
almost impossible for a Republican or a Conservative to
mention the subject without getting into very serious political trouble.

But in 1976 the problem of the massive gap building up
between benefits, and taxes to pay for those benefits, is
bearing down so hard that presidential candidates will
be unable to ignore it. Somewhere along the line, it seems
to me, every candidate—and, of course, everyone in the

Congress—will have to take a stand on one of the following proposals that, at this writing, have been suggested for patching up the old-age plan:

1. Drastically reduce benefit increases.

2. Delay the age at which retirees can receive government pensions.

3. Boost the payroll tax for Social Security, which already is the fastest growing tax in the nation, and in some cases, is larger than the federal income tax.

4. Eliminate the Social Security tax entirely and pay for benefits out of general federal revenues, thus putting the burden of larger pensions on wealthier individuals and corporations.

Any politician worth the name will tell you that the above list presents very difficult choices. No matter which plan he votes for to keep Social Security alive, he is certain to arouse the animosity and opposition of millions of voters. The reaction could go beyond opposition in a passive political sense, for this is the kind of emotional issue that brings out the pickets with their placards and their shouting, the kind that no candidate for president wants to face in even the best of economic periods. And when the unemployment rate is heavy and inflation is running high, I can assure you it is the kind of issue about which politicians have nightmares.

Less than four decades from now—around 2010—those born during the World War II "baby boom" will reach sixty-five years of age, and the number of people collecting government pensions will suddenly jump from 29 million to 45 million, for a 55 percent increase. This will have a devastating impact on the retirement program.

And if you think there is a generation gap plaguing our society now over such things as music, hairstyles, communications, lifestyles, and so forth, just wait until the gap includes the pocketbook. The younger people will be forced to support their elders, just as they have done since the system became law in 1935. But by 2010 the cost could be out of all proportion to the workers' ability to pay. I'm sure I don't have to explain that today's inflation is creating a crisis in the American society that is real and dangerous and frightening. This is not one of those crises manufactured by the politicians and the bureaucrats to get votes. This one is real, and most of you will live to see that I am right. When the *Washington Star,* in an excellent series of articles on Social Security, called the situation a "time bomb," it hit the nail right on the head.

Some observers tell us that if there is indeed a Social Security crisis, it will be an actuarial, not a human, crisis. These are just words and they certainly don't ease my mind. Social Security is on a track which can turn it into a government-built monster that will not only devour wages at an appalling rate but could further slow the workers' initiative, which is even now at a dangerous low.

Social Security is a question with which I have had a great deal to do, especially as it applies to the Great American Game of politics. In the 1960s, in a philosophical discussion with some reporters about political ideology, I said it was too bad that, when Social Security was first made into law, Americans were not given the option of refusing to participate in the program if they so desired. They could then use the money which is now being withheld from their earnings in any way they saw fit. I mentioned that some might have thought they could get a better arrangement through an insurance company. I also pointed out that those who wanted to squander their money in riotous living should have the right to do so, since the money came from their own individual efforts.

This seemingly harmless little conversation rapidly became a national issue once I announced my candidacy for the presidency on the Republican ticket. Liberals in both major parties quickly accused me of wanting to abolish Social Security altogether in a heartless display of callousness towards our older citizens.

It never ceases to amaze me when I recall the people in the media who opposed me and everything I stood for with such vehemence. Some of them actually believed that I would like to hurt "the little man," see him starve or, at the very least, make sure he did not receive what was rightfully his if it in any way got in the way of big business.

Of course, the charge that I wanted to abolish Social Security had no basis in fact. I like to think that I possess as much compassion for my fellowman as anyone else— certainly as much as the liberals who are pounding the taxpayer into the ground with more and more burdensome taxes. But by the time I had been nominated by the Republican convention, I'm sure that to the elders of our country I was the most frightening candidate ever seen on the political horizon. I'm sure most of my readers remember those television commercials showing two hands cutting up a Social Security card and suggesting that this is what would happen if I were elected president.

A few weeks prior to election day Theodore H. White, author of *The Making of the President,** visited my press secretary Tony Smith and said, "What are your people going to do about the Social Security issue? This whole

*New York: Atheneum, 1965.

country is beginning to believe Senator Goldwater wants to abolish the whole system." When Tony asked White what he would do in my place, even if he had $100 million and the entire resources of Madison Avenue at his disposal, White just looked at him and said, "I guess there is nothing anyone can do about a national frame of mind."

I mention this incident to show what a good job my opponents had done in convincing a majority of Americans that I was opposed to help for the aged. Though nothing was further from the truth, I could never make my voice heard above the lies.

Now twelve years have passed, and I really do think it is time that we finally took a good hard look at Social Security. *Please note that I did not say abolish it*—although such a move is fast becoming popular with the younger people, many of whom believe they can better invest this money for their future in their own way.

Do I think we should do away with Social Security at this time? Well, read on and let's see what could be done if we came to that kind of a decision and wanted to make triple sure that none of our older citizens were cheated or hurt.

Theoretically, the billions of dollars which you and I have paid into a trust fund are supposed to be safely held in some place known only to the administrators of the program. I must say that I have not been able to find anyone who can tell just where that one place is or where the fund's money is invested.

Perhaps the biggest problem is that Social Security has become a mixture of welfare and insurance programs. In all events, we now are at the point where major changes are needed, and I do not mean just tinkering around the edges of the system.

What is imperative right now are some basic structural alterations if the Social Security system is to survive as a viable instrument for aiding American workers after they have reached the age of sixty-five. New and important factors have entered the picture since Social Security was established in the 1930s. For example, when the program was first set up very few married women were in the work force. Today there are 22 million married female workers in the United States, and their treatment under the Social Security program is grossly inequitable.

Also, in the 1930s the objective of Social Security was to provide a minimum income for those persons who were subject to the "personal hazards of life," such as old age. Today there are new federal welfare programs which overlap Old Age, Survivors, and Disability Insurance, and the confusion and red tape these have generated is almost unbelievable.

In fact, unless structural changes are soon made to separate the "insurance" from the "welfare" aspects of the federal operation, the expansion of the Social Security program will be completely out of control. From 1965 to 1974 the average monthly benefits for retired workers increased 123 percent—much more than the 56 percent increase in consumer prices. This is the most important reason for the current concern over Social Security's actuarial problems.

One plan for changing the system—suggested by such experts as Prof. James M. Buchanan of the Virginia Polytechnic Institute and State University and Prof. Colin D. Campbell of Dartmouth College—would be to create a program that can be integrated with private programs to provide for one's retirement.

We might even see the day—and not too far off—when this country will have no Social Security program at all. I believe ways and means could be found to close out this program without injuring a single person and without cheating a single worker who has paid into it during his employed years.

As a matter of fact, Prof. Milton Friedman, a widely respected economist of the University of Chicago, and a long-standing friend, already is thinking along these lines. Several years ago, when he participated in a debate at the American Enterprise Institute with Prof. Wilbur J. Cohen, Professor Friedman outlined a program to "wind down" the Old Age, Survivors, and Disability Insurance program. He believes this can be done without injustice to the persons presently covered by taking the following actions:

1. Repeal the payroll tax.

2. Terminate any further accumulation of benefits.

3. Enact a negative income tax, treating payments under Social Security as income for purposes of determining eligibility for benefits.

4. Continue to pay all existing beneficiaries the amounts they are entitled to under current law, except that these amounts should automatically be escalated over time by any changes in the cost of living. This will meet our commitments in real, not nominal, terms. Give such beneficiaries an option to accept a capital sum equal to the present value of the payments instead of continuing payments.

5. Give every worker who has earned coverage under present law a commitment to the retirement and survivors' benefits that he would be entitled to under present law, given his present tax payments and earnings record. This commitment would be in the form of *either* a promise to pay the specified annual sum at the future date when, under present law, he would be entitled to the sum; *or* in

government bonds equal in market value to the present value of those benefits, calculated at the market interest rate on government obligations of corresponding maturity, at the option of the worker.

6. Give every worker who has had taxes paid on his behalf, but has not yet earned coverage, a capital sum equal to the accumulated value of the taxes that have been paid on his behalf.

7. Finance payments under 4, 5, and 6 out of general tax funds, plus the issuance of government bonds.

The reader will notice that in the main these steps recognize and allow for the funding of operations that now exist, though in an unfunded form. They do not add in any way to the true debt of the government by simply putting a stop to the piling up of any further obligations. In addition, these steps would enable the bulk of the present Social Security administrative apparatus to be dismantled almost at once; all that would have to be retained would be a reduced staff to administer step number 4.

I believe such a "winding down" of Social Security would eliminate the present obstacles encountered by persons sixty-five years and over who still want to work, and so would mean a larger national income. It would add to individual savings and mean a higher rate of capital formation and a more rapid rate of income growth. It would stimulate the development and expansion of private pension plans, thereby adding to the security of the workers.

What I'm saying is that if we could find some way to cut down the Old Age, Survivors, and Disability Insurance program, we could promote the general growth of the private sector of the economy. Some preliminary work by Prof. Martin Feldstein of Harvard University suggests the Social

Security system is reducing private savings (and therefore capital formation) in the United States by as much as 30-50 percent of what it otherwise would be.

It strikes me that if these preliminary findings of Prof. Feldstein are anywhere near correct, this is indeed a serious matter, for it gives the Social Security administrators a powerful influence over the nation's economy as well as over the lives of its older citizens. The system is simply an intergenerational transfer program taking money from wage earners in the form of Social Security taxes and transferring it to current Social Security recipients in the form of pension payments. Most of this money is immediately spent by the recipients, so you have a situation whereby taxes on the employer and employee erode the amount available for private savings. By contrast, contributions made to private programs are invested in debt and equity securities and thus contribute to capital formation and economic growth.

Here again, then, we have a government system which literally holds in its power the personal survival of the individual American citizen. As I have pointed out, there are ways to change this situation, but I have been in Congress too long to expect the needed action to come about unless the public demands it. This means that only you, the reader—the American citizen—can make it happen. Think about it.

Before closing this chapter, I think it is well worth noting some additional views expressed by economist Milton Friedman.

In response to my request for his thoughts on Social Security at the present time, Friedman took my questions on the old-age assistance plan several steps further, saying that he believes the fundamental problem facing the American people is the "enormous growth of total government expenditures of all kinds."

"From this point of view," he added, "it may be that the funds drained off by Social Security are doing less harm than they would if they were being spent on multifarious other projects that government has in mind, of which socialized medicine is, at the moment, the most obvious and the most prominent."

He went on to contend that the survival of our free society "to even as limited an extent as it is now free, critically depends on our ability to end the growth in government spending as a fraction of income."

In short, Friedman doesn't believe that the growth in government spending can be halted or cut back by attacking specific programs, whether it be Social Security or any other. He thinks this curtailment can be accomplished only by adopting a constitutional amendment that sets a maximum limit on government expenditures as a percentage of federal income.

IX / The Rush to Reform

In recent months there has been more agitation than ever before in our history for measures to cut down the size, the authority, and the red tape of the federal bureaucracy.

It is encouraging to find the president of the United States leading the campaign for less regulation and less interference by the government in the lives of the American people. Hopefully this will be translated in the near future into some kind of meaningful legislation and federal orders.

However, the "rush to reform" must be a lot more than high-flown rhetoric, vote-getting campaign speeches, and cozy meetings between the president and the federal regulators. It shouldn't be forgotten that in the 1950s, during a similar period of disenchantment with the government bureaucracy, President Eisenhower pledged to cut down or eliminate agencies performing nonessential services that were so costly to the American taxpayer, and issued an executive order freezing the number of federal departments and bureaus. But if Ike ever tried to implement that order, the effort apparently was not good enough. In any case, the intent of the order was quickly forgotten during the Kennedy–Johnson years, which culminated in the enormous and largely useless extravagance of the so-called War on Poverty. Consequently, since the Eisenhower order was issued, more than 220 new agencies have been created and only 21 old ones have been disbanded.

And the pursuit of power in government goes on unabated, even though most American problems can be traced to the abuse of the authority which should belong to the people. It's like a contagious disease which has run a disastrous course in the executive branch of government and is now beginning to affect the Congress.

The chairmen of committees and subcommittees of the Senate and House, as well as their staffs, appear to be superconscious of the power they wield over important legislation. They seem determined to regulate the lives and activities of American citizens in almost every area of human endeavor. Since 1962 the Congress has passed more than twenty-five measures calling for new regulations on the American people and American business, and these programs have increased the costs, the paperwork, and the inflationary pressures on the entire nation.

Meanwhile, power brokers in the Senate and House have used their influence to grind axes for special interests they favor. For example, at the end of the 93rd Congress I was witness to the procedure used to write some tax loopholes into law. It went like this:

Within the last few hours of the session, Chairman Russell Long of the Senate Finance Committee called up a bill which all the Senate members thought had to do solely with providing some relief for the families of veterans, since its title was as tender as a mother's love—"To Provide Tax Relief to the Families of Prisoners of War or Our Fighting Men Listed as Missing in Action." Naturally, every member with an ounce of compassion would want to vote for such a bill.

I know I did—that is, until I got a look at the twelve committee amendments that had somehow gotten attached to the POW tax bill. I found they had nothing to do with the main title or the subject of the bill, but were instead tax loopholes carved out especially for preferred people. One extended to distilled spirits brought into the United States from Puerto Rico and the Virgin Islands the same refund provisions, in the case of loss or destruction, that are presently applicable to imported or domestic spirits.

This is a typical example of how some committee chairmen work. The bill had remained on the calendar from July 8 but was not called up until the last moments of the session in late December when it was believed that not many members would be in attendance and the ones remaining would be anxious to leave.

The point I want to make is this: Those amendments could not have been added to the bill without the knowledge of the committee's chairman because they were committee amendments. But they were added and the Senate was all set to approve them until I objected.

Here we have a small group of men with a flair for getting reelected and a desire for power that can make a mockery on Capitol Hill of the concept of a representative democracy. These are men who run the Congress. They are the chairmen of almost every important committee and subcommittee of the Senate and House. They decide what bills should be brought to the floor for action and when they should be brought to a vote. They also decide exactly what should be contained in every bill submitted for action.

They can ignore bills referred to their committee or they can go through the motions of considering them— that is, give the bills a couple of days of hearings, follow that with a staff report that takes many weeks to write, and then forget the whole thing.

Another prime example of this kind of tactic was in connection with the Federal Elections Campaign Reform Act of 1974. At the time it passed, I said it was one of the worst laws the Congress had ever placed on the statute books. Nevertheless, the supporters of the bill—the people who support Common Cause, the League of Women Voters, and similar groups—hailed it as a major step toward taking the influence of big money out of politics. Now that a little time has passed, however, these groups have discovered that their favorite bill contains a little something extra for incumbent congressmen, senators, and presidential candidates because, as the *Washington Post* noted, the new law made clear that surplus campaign funds can be used by a candidate for which they were raised in almost any way he determines.

The old law, which was supposed to be so faulty, at least had the dubious merit of being ambiguous about the legality of using surplus campaign funds to pay office expenses. That is no longer the case. The way the new law reads—and Fred Wertheimer of Common Cause is the authority for the statement—"slush funds" are now legitimate in American politics. The language in the new bill is so broad that some experts believe a candidate could use any leftover money after the campaign to build himself a house.

Another little-noticed amendment to the new campaign law makes a mockery of the use of the word "reform" in connection with it. This provision shortens the present statute of limitation for campaign violations, and makes the time limit applicable retroactively. Previously, the statute of limitations for prosecution of campaign-spending violations had been five years. But the new provision cuts the limit to three years and applies it in this language:

"No person shall be prosecuted, tried, or punished for violation (of the act) unless the indictment is found or the information is instituted within three years after the date of the violation."

The *Washington Star* said that until recently, Democratic National Chairman Robert Strauss had been under investigation by the Special Prosecutors Task Force on Campaign Finances in connection with a $50,000 cash contribution to the parties from Ashland Oil, Incorporated for the 1972 presidential campaign. What the shortened statute of limitations means is that now the federal prosecutors will not have time to prepare their case against Strauss, or another one against Rep. Wilbur D. Mills (D–Ark.) for a similar allegation of irregular fund-raising, and therefore may very well have to drop the charges against both men.

The *Washington Star* also reported that the shorter statute of limitations was included in the bill at the insistence of two powerful House Democrats—Rep. Phillip Burton of California and Rep. Wayne Hayes of Ohio.

Now that the deficiencies of the new campaign law have been uncovered, the Common Cause organization is right up there among its most vocal critics. If the Common Cause officials had spent as much time studying the campaign bill while it was going through the Congress as they are now spending in criticizing it, perhaps the bill's shortcomings would have been rectified.

The people running the congressional committee should also have been on the lookout for any devious action by the bill's proponents. By this time, it certainly is no secret that the tail end of a congressional session is the lobbyists' best time to accomplish their purposes, and a bill of this nature would be doubly subject to the kind of chicanery I am discussing.

If I had been chairman of the committee that wrote that bill, I would have posted a guard with a shotgun over it until the time an agreement was reached that made some kind of sense.

All elections to federal office now come under the control of the federal government, thanks to the Federal Election Campaign Reform Act of 1974. This law does the following:

—Limits the amount of money an individual can contribute to a political candidate.

—Limits the amount of money an individual can spend —out of his own pocket—on his own political campaign.

—Requires records to be kept of every political contribution over $10; in addition, the name, address, and occupation of every contributor giving more than $100 must be reported to the federal government.

—Sets up a Federal Election Commission, under control of the president and Congress, which has the power to disqualify any candidate it considers to be in violation of this law.

Since monetary contributions are the only way some individuals can participate in an election, this law violates the First Amendment guarantee of free speech. It prevents an individual from having a fair chance to unseat an incumbent by setting maximum campaign-spending limits far below what every empirical study (and experience) indicates is necessary for a challenger's success. It discriminates against the individual in favor of aggregate economic interests by providing loopholes through which "political committees" can proliferate themselves into quasi-separate units, thereby channeling multiple contributions to the same candidate. It allows candidates to spend surplus campaign funds, paid for by the public, on personal expenses. It violates the right of privacy by requiring records to be kept of all but the most minimal campaign contributions. (NOTE: The Nixon White House "enemies list" was compiled from a list of Democratic campaign contributors.) This law prevents political parties which run a candidate in less than ten states from receiving public campaign funds.

And another kind of rush to reform—an overweaning desire to be ultraprotective of the American people—has itself brought on some of the federal agencies' more deadening regulations and controls.

As I mentioned earlier, the government, through the Food and Drug Administration, controls the research and clinical testing of all new drugs developed by private industry. After the 1962 amendments to the Food and Drug Act were passed, companies were required not only to prove their drugs "safe" before they were allowed on the market, but "effective" as well.

The effectiveness of a drug was once a decision left to the individual doctor and his patient. Drugs do not react the same on all people—what may harm one, may heal another. The FDA, however does not recognize this conditional aspect of biochemistry. If a drug is harmful to one person, it is banned from the market for everyone. There is no conditional release for new drugs.

Several years ago the FDA commissioned the National Academy of Sciences to review all drugs marketed in the United States and to classify them according to three categories of effectiveness. Any drug the NAS found to be "ineffective" would be recalled from the market. In 1973, *Private Practice* magazine sent out a questionnaire to 11,000 doctors, asking them to rate twenty-five randomly chosen drugs listed as "possibly effective" by the NAS review. Most of the drugs had been prescribed recently by the doctors, 97 percent of whom said they were effective for their patients in their practice. Yet, because 3 percent of the physicians did not make a similar response, these drugs were scheduled to be withdrawn from the market by the FDA.

The FDA also controls the prescribing pattern of certain drugs—another area traditionally determined by individual physicians and their patients. Recently the FDA moved to control the prescribing of two widely used tranquilizers—Lithium and Valium. Under proper medical supervision, these two drugs have been associated with so few physical problems and side effects that they are considered virtually harmless by most doctors. The FDA, however, had received reports that some patients with suicidal tendencies had killed themselves with overdoses of these drugs; therefore, the agency decided that Lithium and Valium were being abused and overprescribed, and it has now made it illegal for doctors to issue more than a six-month prescription of either drug at one time.

The rush to reform designed to abolish pollution and protect the consumer has added immeasurably to the size of the federal bureaucracy, which was already so large it couldn't be precisely defined. These new agencies have burdened small business to a point where many owners of such enterprises have been driven into bankruptcy. Hence the agencies have thrust the hand of the federal government even deeper into the affairs of the American people.

Students of government affairs talk of the "new regulators" as the operators of a new "managerial revolution" in America. The last such revolution was defined by Adolf Berle and G. C. Means in 1932 in a book entitled *The Modern Corporation and Private Property*. The Berle–

Means revolution was based on the contention that the control of many large industrial corporations has passed from the hands of the owners into those of a small management group. This time, according to economist Murray Weidenbaum, the shift is from professional management selected by a corporation's board of directors to the vast cadre of government regulators.

And the change is costing the consumer money and personal freedom.

For example, as we saw in Chapter IV, pollution-control regulations demanded by the Environmental Protection Agency increased the cost of every new passenger car in 1974 by approximately $320. And though the environmentalists in EPA do not comprise the whole story by any means, there is no doubt that they are striving mightily to create a bureaucratic empire.

Among the other new regulators is the Consumer Products Safety Commission. CPSC has jurisdiction over more than 10,000 products and processes, and possesses the authority to set mandatory safety standards, to ban or recall products from the marketplace without a court hearing, to require product warnings by manufacturers, to order rebates to consumers, and even to send offending executives to jail.

Rep. Jamie Whitten, chairman of the House Appropriations Subcommittee on Consumer Protection, was astounded upon learning of the power held by the relatively new CPSC. In a recent hearing he told the chairman of the consumers' group:

"You've got so much power here it's unbelievable. . . . You've got the power of life or death over whether consumers are to have anything to consume."

There is little likelihood that the CPSC would use the

full extent of its power—but the mere fact that it exists is awesome. And current plans for the new agency are far from reassuring. Professor Weidenbaum, for example, claims the CPSC is planning to declare the average residence an "unsafe product" and thus bring the entire home under the agency's jurisdiction.

Chairman Richard O. Simpson of CPSC—at least in his public statements—obviously isn't reaching for better business–government relations. Take this assertion, for instance:

"If a company violates our statute, we will not concern ourselves with its middle-level executives; we will put the chief executive in jail. Once we put a top executive behind bars, I am sure that we will get a much higher degree of compliance from other companies."

There can be no doubt that officials connected with this new and little-known agency are part of the most powerful independent regulatory agency ever created. And there is little doubt that the tremendous increase in demand for information from the federal government stems from this agency. In its first major proposed rule in August 1973, the CPSC called upon every manufacturer, distributor, or retailer—upon learning that a product it sold had a risk of injury—to provide the commission with a staggering amount of data. Among other things asked for were: the number of products which present a hazard or semihazard; the number of units of each product involved; the number of units of each product in the hands of consumers; specific dates when faulty units were manufactured and distributed and an accounting of when and where such products (and the number units of each) were distributed; the model and serial numbers affected; a list of names and addresses of every distributor, retailer, and producer of the product, if known; a description of the effort that has been made to notify consumers of the defects; and details of corrective tests, quality controls, and engineering changes that were made or contemplated.

In addition, the commission shifts to the manufacturer the full burden of determining and remedying potential product defects, while in the background there is the ever-present threat of criminal sanctions should the commission disagree with the company's decision.

There obviously has been no effort to figure out what the effect might be upon the targets of the agency's actions. For example, the commission has indicated that it ultimately may require manufacturers to keep records of all the product complaints they receive and to make them available to the commission upon request.

Just to give you an idea of the cost factors involved, let me point out that the cost of recalling General Motors products owned by some 6.5 million people amounts to $3.5 million for the mailing alone.

In any event, the relatively new consumer-safety operation will require a major record-keeping effort so that owners of a recalled product can be promptly notified. Also, an expansion of service firms would be necessary to replace the faulty parts.

There probably has never been a regulatory agency established in the federal government which practiced more high-handedness from the very beginning than the CPSC. One of its first cases, in which the agency revealed an excess of bureaucratic zeal or just plain bad judgment, involved the ordering of formal hearings to determine if four million electric frying pans were hazardous.

The fascinating aspect of this case is that out of these four million frying pans, not a single injury had been reported to the commission. Murray Weidenbaum, in reporting on the CPSC's action, stated: "It is no exaggeration to suggest that the commission—unwittingly, of course —may turn out to be the most anti-consumer organization of all time."

It's amazing to me that the Consumer Products Safety Commission has been so little publicized. I believe the main reason for this is that the Environmental Protection Agency got most of the attention. However, we are due to hear a great deal more about CPSC and another new agency— the Occupational Safety and Health Administration. Nobody could overlook the OSHA, because it is that part of the federal government which makes sure that the cuspidors are cleaned daily in the federal establishments.

In the new period of U.S. regulation, the Occupational Safety and Health Administration comes in for a great deal of attention. It is one of those agencies whose objectives are so worthy that anyone who questions them runs the risk of being called a hard-hearted partisan completely lacking in human compassion. After all, who isn't in favor of improving work environments in which 14,000 Americans were killed in 1975 in job-related accidents?

Even so, the worth of its objective doesn't stop OSHA from ridiculous conduct, such as the promulgation of stupid rules. Even the Federation of American Scientists was moved in 1973 to issue a critical description of the way OSHA operated. It made the following statement:

"Regulations are voluminous and complex: the language is convoluted beyond recognition except by a scientist or lawyer. Worse yet, there is no provision for a penalty-free consultation with an Occupational Safety and Health Administration inspector. . . .

"The Occupational Safety and Health Act, in short, has created at least as many problems as it was designed to solve."

(Right here it should be explained that the Federation of American Scientists is entirely sympathetic with the OSHA's rule calling for the daily cleaning of spittoons.)

The agency has gone overboard on the subject of rules and regulations. Some are so long and tedious that the agency's own representatives aren't always familiar with them. As a case in point, when Professor Weidenbaum sent a research assistant to check on the order relating to spittoons, he was assured by the area representative that no such provision existed. But the OSHA regulations published in the *Federal Register* contain the following statement: "Cuspidors are considered undesirable but, if used, they shall be of such construction that they are cleanable. They will be cleaned at least daily when in use (Title 29, Section 1910, (A) (Z) (ii))."

As minor as this incident is, it nonetheless bothers me because it points up the ease with which federal officials deny, lie, or brush off embarrassing questions from the people who pay their salaries and who worry about others who do the same. What's more, it strikes me that if federal officials can fabricate untrue stories about something as foolish as cuspidors, there is no telling what they could do about more important items owned by the federal government.

Regardless, the toughest criticism of OSHA has not come from businessmen or labor, but from the federal government itself. One of its toughest critics is Chairman Robert D. Moran of the Occupational Safety and Health Review Commission. This is an independent agency created to hear appeals from rulings by OSHA inspectors.

Moran claims too many standards are (to paraphrase Winston Churchill) "riddles, wrapped in mysteries inside enigmas. They don't give the employer even a nebulous suggestion of what he should do to protect his employees from whatever it is (also left unexplained) which represents a hazard to their safety and health."

After citing one vague and general standard, Moran declared:

"I submit that there isn't a person on earth who can be certain he is in full compliance with the requirements of this standard at any particular point of time."

So far as small business is concerned, interpretation of OSHA's standard is the big problem. Since small businessmen are unable to employ experts to explain bureaucratic regulations, they usually go to the government for help. When they go to OSHA, however, they get material they can't understand or material they don't need. One document suggested by the OSHA guide contains 455 pages of fine print, including algebraic and trigonometric equations. But if someone skips that part of the instruction, he can make the discovery elsewhere in the guide that a ladder is "an appliance usually consisting of two side rails joined at regular intervals by cross pieces called steps, rungs, cleats, on which a person may step in ascending or descending."

And if the person is interested in the hazards that may be related to his departure from a building, he can learn all about the word "exit." The guide tells him that "exit is that portion of a means of egress which is separated from all other spaces of the building or structure by construction or equipment as required in this subpart to provide a protected way of travel to the exit discharge. A means of egress is a continuous or unobstructed way of exit travel

from any point in a building or structure to a public way
and consists of three separate and distinct parts: the way
of exit access, the exit, and the way of exit discharge. A
means of egress comprises the vertical and horizontal ways
of travel and shall include intervening room spaces, door-
ways, hallways, corridors, passageways, balconies, ramps,
stairs, enclosures, lobbies, escalators, horizontal exits, and
courts and yards."

The trouble with OSHA regulations, according to Moran,
is that many of them are so lacking in uniformity that the
agency workers themselves can't tell anyone how to comply
with them, for they are not in a position to know if and
when regulations have been violated.

Among other things wrong with the Occupational Safety
and Health Act is that no provision is made for "courtesy
inspections." In other words, a company invites OSHA inspectors to look at its operations at its own peril. Instead
of receiving information on what the government wants,
such invitations can easily result in instant citations for
some infraction of OSHA rules and regulations. One would
think the government would welcome voluntary requests
from business firms seeking to know if their facilities
measure up to federal standards. This doesn't seem to be
the case, however.

One other factor, important to the big businessman as
well as to his smaller counterpart, is cost. In some cases,
safety and health investments are a significant part of an
industry's total capital spending. For instance, in 1972,
almost 8 percent of the textile industry's investments and
10 percent of the steel industry's outlays went for health
and safety equipment.

According to estimates by McGraw-Hill's Department of
Economics, upcoming industrial investments in health and

safety equipment are expected to rise from $2.5 billion in 1972 to $3.4 billion in 1977. But in a recent study commissioned by OSHA, it was estimated that the cost to American industry of bringing existing facilities into compliance with current OSHA noise standards of 90A Scale decibels will total $13.5 billion.

Figures like these, thrown around by OSHA, are building a fire in Congress to require "economic impact" statements to be published in conjunction with new regulatory standards. At long last, it seems, the congressmen are beginning to see the importance of having agencies attach price tags to their requests as well as estimates of future costs.

When I think about how government bureaucracies operate, I am always reminded of that fine segment in John F. Kennedy's inaugural speech, when he said, "Ask not what your country can do for you but what you can do for your country." Washington is full of groups or individuals that are forever coming up with ways in which the country can do *to* you or *for* you with your money. Those interested in reform should demand an end to this now before our lives are totally dominated by Washington.

Conclusion

Before closing, I would like to reemphasize that when power is used to deprive people of their freedoms, it makes no difference where it accumulates. This is what I have attempted to show in this book.

Power lodged in hidden recesses of government and vested in unknown bureaucrats can sometimes be as important as that wielded by a heavily partisan Congress or a power-hungry president. It is the power *per se*—the authority—the official influence—that counts; and in my opinion that even includes the power *not* to use the power in our national interest.

Because of the long lead time required by publishers for the preparations of a finished book, I am writing this conclusion on one of the saddest days in American history. It is the day a nation fell because of American failure to honor its commitments to an ally.

And I find myself actually wondering whether the events we are living through tonight spell the collapse of the American position in the international field, the collapse of that benevolent position that has preserved international peace in most of the world since World War II.

This is a situation where the power not to use power comes into the picture. Could we have won the war in Vietnam if our military men had been given permission to do so? There is no question but that we could have. So what went wrong?

The trouble was that civilians who have constitutional power refused—yes, refused—to allow our military units to do what had to be done. In one of the few times in our history the civilians at home charted every move for our army, navy, air force, and marines.

This infamy (and that's my word for it when American boys are dying) kept us from winning a war. It was embodied in a book of rules which day after day went from Washington to the commanders in the field. And the *power*? It was exerted in the names of two commanders-in-chief and one secretary of defense.

In these pages, we have been dealing with a comparable but nevertheless different subject—the lodgement, exercise, and abuse of power here at home. As I worked on the manuscript, it became clear to me that the great majority of the American people have no accurate picture whatsoever of just what is going on in their government. They are totally unaware of the coming breakpoint. Let me give a few statistics that, hopefully, may shock some readers into a realization of how far things have gone in the Republic.

For every dollar we pay in income tax in 1976, the government will borrow fifty cents. Two hundred years ago the United States began this process—and here I'm talking about borrowing—to win their freedom. At that time we borrowed $8 million to finance our revolution.

Today that debt is 76,000 times greater. It is being used for a phenomenal increase in the cost of operating the Congress and implementing the sweeping powers given to that faceless army making up the regulatory agencies which tell the American people what they can and cannot do in most of the important areas of their everyday lives. The debt is being used to finance a growing, unworkable, and destructive welfare system which has not solved any problems—but has created many. And it is increasing the threat of a breakpoint.

The increased debt, of course, defrays the cost of the greatest bureaucracy—with all of its waste, inefficiency, and duplication—the world has ever seen. It pays for a government work force (federal) of 2,710,536 people, the largest salaried group anywhere in the nation or in the world. (In the Department of Agriculture alone, there are 105,907 employees; this means one government worker for every 26.6 farmers in the nation.) In 1974 the cost of paying this work force was $33 billion and the average individual salary was $12,200.

This money also pays for 800 chauffeured automobiles used by top federal officials, and covers the cost of the Library of Congress' 320 miles of shelves which contain the wisdom, knowledge, and experience of civilization. More than 4,200 experts, paid from these funds, assist individuals in getting what they need from 16 million books and 58 million other published items contained in the Library.

The debt helps maintain 300,000 buildings to which Uncle Sam holds title in the United States and around the world. It also keeps in operation some 26,000 computers, from the largest, most sophisticated machine available to the smallest.

The increasing machinery helps account for some of the $16 billion a year required just to handle the federal government's paperwork "blizzard" for one year which, as mentioned earlier, may have something to do with our cloak-and-dagger operations at the Pentagon. Conservative estimates place the amount of secret papers shredded by the Department of Defense each day at sixteen tons.

More and more I believe that we are in a period which Thomas Jefferson would have described as one requiring a revolution to restore the principles of the American Revolution. In his inaugural address, Jefferson called for a return to the Spirit of 1776, and said the general government must be preserved in "its whole Constitutional vigor, as the sheet anchor of our peace at home and our safety abroad."

Although Jefferson was referring to situations that existed in the United States of his day, I believe there is in his words a strain of wisdom that is more applicable to our present state of affairs than most statements I keep hearing in Washington. In fact, I think it is safe to say that more so now than at any other time in our history, we need revolutionary thinking and acting in respect to all segments of government if we are to avoid the breakpoint.

America today has grave and growing problems and invariably we treat them in the wrong sequence. Current discussions, for example, always center around inflation, recession, unemployment, energy, and pollution. Almost never does anyone bring up Problem Number One—the maintenance of public order. And without order, we can do nothing. Without order, none of our solutions are worth a damn because we can't even begin to implement them.

America's rising crime rate is directly related to the loss of order in populated sections of the United States. And the reason for this is that we have a *negative power* in operation—the power of indifference on the part of the American people. The price we pay for this indifference is permissiveness in all areas of human endeavor.

In modern America even the criminal has his share of

power. When the criminal's power isn't being used directly in the commission of a murder, rape, burglary, or mugging, it is intimidating a large part of the population. Millions of free citizens are afraid to exercise their liberties for fear of being overpowered by killers, thugs, and thieves.

I can remember the days in the early 1930s when I worked in New York City. Then we walked all over the city, from Greenwich Village to Harlem, from the East Side to the West Side and any other place we wanted to go, without the slightest fear of assault or trouble of any kind. Today, one doesn't dare venture more than a few blocks from where one lives in that great city.

And when I came here to Washington twenty-two years ago, it was my practice to walk every evening, sometimes for five or six miles, visiting neighborhoods and talking to the people. But I can't do that any longer and feel safe. The story is the same all over America, even in my hometown of Phoenix. One is frightened of going out alone at night to visit places that he has known all his life.

But to return to federal power—what about the country? Is the United States doomed to collapse under the weight of deficits resulting from the long contest for power in the federal government?

I certainly don't think the Damoclean threat is immediate, but I do think the nation has less than ten years to function at the current rate of expenditures before the sword descends. I also believe the country is in for some very rough times because of federal economic stupidity.

As I stated at the beginning of this work, our Founding Fathers designed our Constitution and our democratic and republican form of government to guard against the concentration and abuse of power. I admonish the reader now to do as I once did—review the works of the Founding Fathers to become better acquainted with the great limitations they placed on the attempts of any group or person to usurp the power that belongs to the American people. When you have the knowledge and understand it, you can then understand the dangers that presently face this country.

As I also stated at the start, my primary reason for writing this book is to alert Americans to the dangers of power concentrated in any place or in any hands. It is not—to repeat what I've often said during my political career—the concentration of power in foreign countries or any combination of foreign countries that I fear, but the power within our own government's structure that slowly but surely undermines the morality of the people and even their ability to understand what is happening to their freedom before it is all gone. The wrong use of power has destroyed more governments and deprived more people of freedom than has any other action in the history of man. Throughout the course of this book I have mentioned only a few of the abuses that I see from the nation's capital. It has been sort of like skimming the top of the milk; the real substance is way down underneath. I have cited facts and figures, but hundreds of thousands remain unrecorded here. Some rather bizarre and unusual incidents have been noted, but thousands more exist.

If this book does nothing more than whet your appetite for finding out more about the abusive power that has grown in Washington since the early 1930s, then I will consider it a success. It is only when the American people finally come to realize what is happening to the freedoms they have always taken for granted, to the monies they have worked so hard to earn, and to the moral atmosphere of our nation as a result of these abuses that any change will take place in the structure of Congress, so that enough courage can be shown to redirect the course of history which is now headed, in my humble opinion, toward total disaster.

One of the best suggestions I could make to anyone who has proceeded this far in this book is that he go back through the works of Gibbon to where he discusses the decline and fall of the Roman Empire. Or for even easier reading, some of the historical novels by Taylor Caldwell describe the conditions in Rome prior to its collapse. This will give the reader an understanding of what conservatives mean when they stress the admonition, previously quoted, that is inscribed on Washington's National Archives Building: "What is past is prologue—study the past."

If we will remember the lessons of history we can prevent the disasters of history from repeating themselves. And again I remind you, what has happened to this country over the last forty years through the gradual concentration of power in the hands of the bureaucrats in Washington and through the improper use of power, has put this nation into international disrepute and even international trouble.

I have attempted to establish in these pages the points of honor that brought us glory in the past and to describe the kind of power that can eat away and destroy both our honor and the nation's glory. We normally think of power as the nation's ability to get things done both at home and abroad. But when power is distorted and the nation's ability to accomplish things extends to taking from the individual his right to use his own ability to obtain the things he desires and would benefit by, that is something else.

It has taken the United States many years to get into a position where its power so absolutely dominates so many factors of our lives; curtailing that power is not going to be an overnight venture. As matters stand now, we are in about the same position as was Rome before she collapsed, in the same position that Babylon and ancient Greece and the modern countries of Europe found themselves before the freedoms of the people and the powers of the countries disappeared. Some people, in fact too many, go blithely on their way thinking it can't happen here. They have never heard of the breakpoint.

Thus in spite of the fact that Old Glory is still a symbol of everything we hold dear and great in this country, in spite of the fact that every time the flag is paraded down the streets of our towns and cities it brings men to attention and tears to the eyes of those who care—in spite of all of this, the American flag and all it stands for can fall. It can go down even though for two hundred years men have been willing to lay down their lives for the freedoms God has given us and which our constitutional government was set up to protect.

All the way from Valley Forge through the bitterness of the War between the States, through the terrors of World Wars I and II, Korea, and Vietnam, our men have added to the glory of the flag and to the perpetuation and pro-tection of our freedom. The colonists, the pioneers who opened up our frontiers, the men and women who tilled the soil, and those who created our cities—all these were people who cherished that hard-won freedom and conse-quently resisted any offers of so-called government help that would chip away at it. Instead, they depended on their own hard work and personal initiative to make what they wanted of their lives.

This is the kind of glory that built our nation. It is the kind of glory on which we prided ourselves and through which we became mighty throughout the entire world. But despite the triumph of the people over power in the past, the present curses and threats to freedom will not automatically pass. Once men have felt the strength of power they are not likely to give it up voluntarily. It will, I repeat, have to be taken away from them and placed back where it was supposed to reside, and this will happen only when the American people find the courage to elect Congresses that don't hold out glittering promises which, when implemented, simply increase the concentration of bureaucratic power and entangle the people in an even tighter web of dependency on the government. Saying No to any more government "benefits" may mean that our present standard of living will have to be lowered a bit. But if we don't settle for a little less now, we most assuredly will be forced to settle for a great deal less in the not-too-distant future.

Now, as we begin the 200th celebration of the founding of our country, the founding of our constitutional Republic, I think the challenge that faces us all is whether Americans will celebrate the 225th, 250th, 300th, or 500th anniversaries of this country. Or will our children be looking back on the ruins of a once-great concept that died because not enough people cared?

Recently a friend of mine told me that in his stamp-collecting days he purchased an English stamp which carried the familiar slogan, "The sun never sets on the British Empire." But the sun has set on the empire because England allowed herself to become weak, militarily as well as economically. The question that this brings to mind is: Just where is our sun in relation to the United States? Is it at high noon where it should be? Or is it over the yardarm, ready to disappear beyond the horizon?

If darkness comes, it will be because the United States

has lost both its economic and military strength. Our sun can begin to set without external influence. All that is necessary to bring about such a tragedy is the continued apathy of American business people, professionals, and individual citizens, coupled with the unbridled power of government bureaucracies, the labor unions, and special-interest groups.

To sum up, the purpose of this book has been to give the reader and the American public some idea of what this one elected official sees taking place within the structure of our government; for just as surely as I'm writing this, the bureaucratic meddling in our lives can destroy our God-given freedoms and the government set up to protect them almost two hundred years ago. Again, I hope I'm wrong in my pessimism, but history, I'm afraid, could well prove me right. If you have read anything in this book that you find disturbing, I would suggest you discuss it with your neighbors and friends, because only when the American people are aware of what is taking place will they demand change.

Believe me, I know from past experience that when the people get wrought up over a public issue such as runaway federal spending, they make it known to their representatives and senators in Congress. And also believe me when I say that when this happens, you get action from the liberal mandarins who control the Senate and House.

That's what we need right now, so let's get cracking. We have nothing to lose but an army of petty dictators ordering us how to live. The American way of life is at stake, and that's worth fighting for. If we join together in the fight, we can still avoid reaching the breakpoint.

INDEX